The Apparitions
at
Medjugorje Prolonged

by
René Laurentin

A merciful delay for a world in danger?

Translated by
Judith Lohre Stiens

Edited and Published by
THE RIEHLE FOUNDATION
P.O. Box 7
Milford, Ohio 45150

The publisher recognizes and accepts that the final authority regarding the apparitions at Medjugorje rests with the Holy See of Rome, to whose judgment we willingly submit.

—The Publisher

Published by The Riehle Foundation
For additional copies, write:
The Riehle Foundation
P.O. Box 7
Milford, Ohio 45150

This book originally published as *La Prolongation de Apparitions de Medjugorje* December 1986 by O.E.I.L., Paris France.

Library of Congress Catalog Card No. 87-61292

ISBN: 0-9618840-0-2

DEDICATION

The publishing of this English edition is dedicated to the late Raymond R. and Eleanora Riehle, founders of The Riehle Foundation, in recognition of their unwavering devotion to the Mother of God.

The Riehle Foundation
Publisher

TABLE OF CONTENTS

Chapter   Page

Preface vii
Publisher's Forward ix
Introduction xiii
1. The Fifth Anniversary 1
2. How to Paint an Apparition 6
3. News of the Seers 13
   A. Those Who Still See 13
      Jakov 13
      Ivan 14
      Vicka 15
      Maria 18
   B. Those Who No Longer See 20
      Ivanka 20
      Mirjana 24
      Helena Sees Things in a Different Way 35
4. The Parish in Torment 38
   From Fr. Tomislav to Fr. Slavko 38
   And to Fr. Ivan Dugandzic 39
   An Accusation 40
   The Premature Dissolution of the Commission ... 41
5. The Scientific Works 44
   The Latest French and Italian Tests 45
   Insensitivity to Pain 46
   Allusions to Potential Studies 47
   The Rapture Submitted to a Lie Detector Test 50
   The Rapture Above and Beyond
      Pathalogical Prescriptions 52
   Conclusions 53
   Time for the Psychiatrists 55
   Ecclesiastical Statutes of the Scientific
      Contribution 59
6. The Messages 62

The Base Message 62
The Thursday Messages 62
Other Messages 71
7. The Signs 73
The Healings 73
Luminary Phenomenon 75
8. The Fruits 78
The Seers 79
The Charisma of the Second Group,
   Helena and Marijana 80
Helena 81
Prayer Groups 87
The Parish 88
The Pilgrims from the Entire World 90
Testimonies 91
9. Conclusions
   (Where Are We Going Now?) 96
10. The Latest News
   (Up until the beginning of 1987) 98
Regarding the Seers 98
Mirjana 98
Ivanka 98
Ivan 99
Jakov 100
Maria 100
Vicka 101
Other Events 105
The Church's Position on Medjugorje 106
A Special Message 106

PREFACE

The title of this book calls for an explanation.

The 10 secrets received by the seers at Medjugorje are serious. Most of them announce difficulties which weigh on our times. In abandoning ourselves more and more to sin, the world is calling for its own destruction.

According to the seers, and principally Mirjana (who along with Ivanka saw the first apparition), the revelation of 10 secrets will proceed in the following manner:

1. The first two warnings will recall the urgency of conversion. (Several people asked me if the catastrophe at Chernobyl was one of them. The answer is no, because the warnings will be revealed before the event happens. Chernobyl, therefore, could not have been a warning. And the message of Medjugorje is connected more to moral and interior ruin rather than to material menaces.)
2. According to what Mirjana said on October 25, 1985, the visible and permanent sign which will be given on the hill in Medjugorje to persuade the non-believers will constitute the third warning, which is also the third secret.
3. Finally will come the seven remaining secrets of which the last three will be very grave.

After 20 months without an apparition, from December 25, 1982 to August 26, 1984, Mirjana again received some communications (through locutions and some visions) from Our Lady to prepare for the coming revelation of the secrets. One will see how in this book.

"This revelation is near," she said.

After more than one year, astonished that the unveiling had not yet begun, I asked Mirjana about it (as you will be able to read later on in this book). She saw the delay as a period of grace, a time of mercy. And so we have the explanation for our title of the book.

It is necessary to accept it with prudence and reserve. Even if the fruits of the apparitions and other signs assure the authenticity of the supernatural happening, they still do not guarantee the predictions because predictions, always incomprehensible before their realization, are often an ambiguous phenomenon and rarely are they infallible. Even Saints have erred in this area. We have the classic case recorded by spiritual authors of St. Catherine of Siena. She was thought to have received a message according to which the Virgin was not conceived without sin. In the same way, St. Paul and the first Christians believed that the end of the world was very near. Eschatology and predictions can be subject to optical illusions. Is this the case of Medjugorje? And in what measure? Sound judgment obliges us to ask these questions, which in no way hinders the certainty of these occurrences nor diminishes the urgency to convert oneself for the salvation of the world which is in danger.

What is the special characteristic of Medjugorje? I would be tempted to say that there is none, since it is the same Virgin who appeared at La Salette, at Lourdes, at Fatima, and now here. However, there is something special here. There is a cry from Heaven in response to an urgent need of our world which did not exist at the time of Lourdes. This is not so much the danger of war (which does exist), it is rather the urgent need of a world that has given itself up to sin, and has put itself in danger of self-destruction because of sin. The Virgin warns us that we shall not be saved from this situation by magic, by science, or by politics, but only by a return to prayer, conversion, fasting, a new life—salvation comes from within. That is what is happening at Medjugorje.

This latest edition of my book has been updated after my last two trips to Medjugorje, August 12-15 and October 10-15 in 1986, the 11th and the 12th by the author.

PUBLISHER'S FORWARD

BACKGROUND INFORMATION

The place is St. James Parish in the remote village of Medjugorje, Yugoslavia, where it is claimed that the Blessed Virgin Mary has been making almost daily appearances since June 24, 1981. Six teenage children (two boys and four girls) are witness to these appearances which began on a mountain behind the village. The apparition identified herself as the Blessed Virgin Mary, the Queen of Peace. The message she brings is an urgent one for mankind. She stated to the children, "I have come to tell the world that God exists. I am here to tell the world that peace is necessary for the salvation of the world. Mankind must be reconciled with God and with one another. For this to happen, it is necessary to believe, to pray, to repent and to do penance."

THE MESSAGE

The Madonna presents herself as a servant and messenger from God. The messages she brings do not convey any new teachings. They echo the Gospels and teachings of the Church. As at Fatima, they restate the conditions for peace in the world, and for the very existence of the world. The basic message of Medjugorje is: Faith, Peace, Conversion, Prayer, Penance and Fasting. These messages are for the entire world.

THE APPARITIONS

The visionaries see Our Lady as a real three-dimensional person whom they can hear and touch. They describe her as beautiful beyond words, radiant with holiness. Her presence is preceded by a brilliant light. Her conversations with the children take the form of motherly tenderness and concern. She also takes the role of a catechist in advising and directing their lives, and the Church as well.

THE SECRETS

Our Lady told the children that she would impart 10 secrets to all of them. Some of these secrets have to do with the world, some with the local church and parish, some with the Church as a whole. Two of the girls have already received the 10 secrets and no longer see Our Lady with the others. The other seers have all received nine secrets. We are lead to believe that the 9th and 10th secrets speak about punishments for the sins of the world and are very grave.

THE GREAT SIGN

One of the secrets, partially revealed by the children, is that Our Lady has promised to leave a visible sign on the mountain where she first appeared so that the world would believe. The sign will be a testimony and cause for conversion. She said that the sign would be given after the apparitions have ended. Most of the children know what the sign will be and the exact date.

SIGNS AND WONDERS

Unusual events began taking place soon after the first apparition. Many of these have to do with the large cross at the top of Mount Krizevac, the highest peak in the area. (In 1933, a 20 foot cement cross was built on the mountain by the people to commemorate the 1900th year of Our Lord's death and resurrection.) Hundreds have seen the word "MIR" (the Croation word for PEACE) written in large bright letters in the sky above the cross. The cross has been seen to emit a brilliant light. On numerous occasions, thousands have witnessed the sun change colors, spin, become a silver disc, throb and pulsate in the sky, and throw off a rainbow of colors.

Also, there have been over a hundred and fifty claimed physical healings. But the most important healings are the spiritual ones. The deep spiritual conversions, the changing of hearts and lives, is the greatest of all the many "signs" at Medjugorje.

THE CHURCH

The Catholic Church has not yet made an official statement on the claimed apparitions at Medjugorje. Following the closing of a controversial commission study headed by the local Bishop, the Magesterium of the Church in Rome has requested a new commission on a national level to study the events in Medjugorje.

All the appearances of Mary on earth which have been approved by the Church have the following points in common, all of which are present at Medjugorje:

—Mary always calls us back to God, a return to Jesus.
—Mary has always re-affirmed what is already in the Faith and teachings of the Catholic Church.
—Mary has always called us to prayer and sacrifice in reparation for sin, a message of the Gospels.

SUMMARY

St. James Parish in Medjugorje is the center of all activity. All services and devotions center around the Eucharist. Mary affirms this with, "Return to Jesus." Father Tomislav Pervan, the Pastor of St. James, believes God is at work in his parish. He says that, "Through Mary, people find God here in the Mass, in the Sacrament of Reconciliation, a return to Faith that happens to thousands every week; that is the biggest miracle."

The crowds of pilgrims continue to flock to Medjugorje; over five million to date. People of all faiths come and join together in prayer. The teachings of Mary for the past six years in this Communist controlled country have been ecumenical in nature.

The apparitions continue daily; the length of the appearances has become shorter, sometimes with only two or three seers present. They seem to be winding down. But the people still come to this remote mountain village, with very few facilities and very little comfort; and the conversions abound.

THIS BOOK

Since 1981, when the apparitions began, and as the story unfolded, news of the event spread. Over the next several years, numerous books, films and video tapes emerged.

One of the earlier books, "Is the Virgin Mary Appearing at Medjugorje?" was authored by Fr. Rene Laurentin (Word Among Us Press, 1984, 169 pages). We strongly recommend its reading as a total composite of the Medjugorje story. Fr. Laurentin is a theologian of international repute, an author of more than fifty books, and an historian of apparitions. His works are both scholarly and research oriented.

Now, some three years later, he brings us this new update on Medjugorje; a current look at his earlier work. His approach is forceful, direct, sometimes blunt, always analytical. He covers up neither the mystery of grace, nor the doubt. In this most important commentary, he detects the success and the difficulty; and with a deep, burning concern for the Church, and the salvation of mankind. he presents both.

The phenomenon continues; the pilgrims increase (over five million to date). From all countries and all faiths they come, responding to the events unfolding in a remote mountain village, being delivered, presumably, by "The Handmaid of the Lord." —the Madonna of Medjugorje.

We wish to express our deep appreciation to Mrs. Judith Lohre Stiens, of Edgewood, Kentucky, for the English translation of this book ("La Prolongation des Apparitions de Medjugorje," O.E.I.L., Paris, France, Dec. 1986).

We also thank Fr. Francois Pellissier, of the Glenmary Home Missioners, Cincinnati, Ohio, for his invaluable assistance.

INTRODUCTION

The apparitions of Medjugorje have passed their 5th anniversary. Their long duration surprises one: 1,725 apparitions, as the newspapers say. But this number is nothing more than approximate. People speak of five days without apparitions, yet this statement is not well verified. There were often two apparitions in the same day, notably those which took place in the evening on the hill, or one or two times per week in the later years. It would then probably be more accurate to say more than 2,000. Yet, no one has taken a truly accurate count. It is not really of great importance.

This total astonishes us because the apparitions that have been recognized in these last centuries have lasted but a short period: One single time at La Salette (1848); once only at Pontmain (January 17, 1871); 18 apparitions at Lourdes; and 9 at Fatima (counting the ones of the angel in 1916).

If the length and duration of the apparitions at Medjugorje amazes us, around the time of the Middle Ages, certain seers were granted apparitions all their lives without being vocal about it or attracting large crowds.

This great number of apparitions at Medjugorje explains itself by these reasons:

1. It is a pedagogy, a teaching.
2. The message is not made to be written on the walls, but in our lives. Accordingly, we are reminded of the words of St. Paul to the Corinthians. "You are a letter of Christ . . .written not with ink but by the Spirit of the living God, not on tablets of stone but on the tablets of flesh in the heart." (*2 Cor.* 3:3).

The writing of Christ is slow to come into our lives in great depth.

Some people say that these messages are repetitive; that

it is just so much talk, that this is not the style of the Virgin, she is so quiet, or she expresses herself in short sentences in the Gospels (for example *Luke* 1, 38; 46-56; 2, 48; *John* 2, 4). But the repetitions serve the purpose of urging us into putting the messages into practice; to interiorization in our daily life. They are like the words of a mother to her child. If you edited all that a mother says to her child during the first four years of his life, it would be tens of thousands of pages of repetition. It is thanks to this repetition, to these banal daily exchanges, that a child absorbs all these impressions before his fourth year, say the psychologists. As a result, he learns well and speaks his mother language fluently. The foundations of his life are well established on these simple words; words that have been imbedded in him from the beginning. And the repetition of these words is another way of showing maternal love. At Medjugorje, the "Gospa" (Our Lady) acts as a mother.

Other reasons the apparitions have lasted is as a help to those in danger. Such a spiritual event could only make its way slowly under a Communist regime where the diffusion or the spread of these words has been difficult. Even the Bishop of Mostar, Bishop Zanic, though recognizing the fruits and the value of the liturgy, openly declared his intention to snuff out these events. He had announced to visitors, who he received, his negative declaration regarding the apparitions—first in March of 1985 (as he reported in the "Gazette de Venezia"), and then again in May 1986. But it was made difficult for him to reach such a judgment before the ending of the apparitions. And in April 1986, Rome recommended adjournment of the Bishop's investigating committee and the suspension of a final judgment. The prolonging of the apparitions was a decisive obstacle in this negative judgment.

The difficulties that Medjugorje suffers (being located in a Communist controlled state; in a diocese where long standing local quarrels with the Franciscans have made the Bishop hostile; and the nearly impossible material conditions for a pilgrimage) would have normally provoked disorder, battles, insurmountable problems and confusion. But at the price of heavy sacrifices, all these difficulties have been eased through prayer. This is the dominant theme throughout the updated news of events at Medjugorje.

This book is being published at the time when Mirjana is preparing to unveil the secrets. What will they be? We will finish there. This volume will give successively the news on the following points:

1. The fifth anniversary (June 25, 1986).
2. A new painting of the apparition.
3. The Seers.
4. The words of the Commission of Inquiry and the impromptu dissolution by the Bishop on May 2, 1986.
5. The scientific works.
6. The messages.
7. The signs.
8. The fruits.
9. Where do we go from here?
10. Appendix—Latest updates.

(Above) The site of the first apparition is pointed out to us by the sister of Maria, Milka Pavlovic (17 years old), who saw the apparition only on the first day.

"It has been very long ago. Haven't you forgotten?" I said to her.

"That, one never forgets." she answers.

"But after 5 years..." I continued.

"Five years? It is like today." she says.

She saw the Virgin just that one time and only from afar. The next day, the other seers saw the apparition up closer.

(Below) Milka had asked Ivanka and Maria to help her clear away the debris by this road, which leads to the apparition site.

Chapter 1

THE FIFTH ANNIVERSARY

Some people had hoped that the 5th anniversary (June 25, 1986) would be marked by a profound event. Would this be the revelation of the secrets? Would we see once again a sign in the sky? Or the Virgin herself? Nothing came to substantiate these suppositions. The grace of Medjugorje is other than this; it is the intimate rediscovery of God by conversion and in prayer. It is that which characterized the anniversary.

I had arrived June 22, 1986 in the evening, admist the crowds of the big weekend. Traffic was impossible, often blocked, but without shouting or altercations of any kind in all the area that surrounded the church. The houses of the seers were also besieged but in a very calm manner.

The next day, June 23rd, I went to Vicka's home for the apparition. She was recovering from her operation and was not able to kneel down. The Virgin came to her, and she remained standing during the apparition. It was very short. I was sorry and wondered if it was my fault because, for a long time, I had wanted for a deaf mute to read Vicka's lips during the conversations she had with the apparition. Just as in January 1985, when Dr. Frigerio had equipped Vicka with a laryngophone which would have permitted the decifering of sounds during the apparition, it, too, was exceptionally brief, around 10 seconds. This experiment was not repeated.

Vicka, whose patience, so contrary to her temperament, had become inexhaustible, greeted us with a smile and answered our questions on the brevity of this apparition.

The crowd of the weekend (Sunday, June 22) stayed on through Monday the 23rd and grew still larger for the anniversary of the first two days of the apparitions (Monday, June 24, and Tuesday, June 25).

How many were there? All one knows is that it was a great crowd, and one that had grown since the spring of 1985; Italians and Croations mostly. For the concelebration of the Mass on

1

Jakov during the fifth anniversary apparition.

June 24, 1985 (4th anniversary), there were 60 priests of which 40 were Italian. June 24, 1986, there were 120 priests of which 97 were Italian. There must have been in excess of 60,000 people there, clearly more than in 1985.

The continuation of the pilgrimages has prompted construction and commerce around the village. There were practically no merchants before 1985. Today stalls and little prefabricated shops now total about 20. The purchase of fresh drinks is available at the foot of the path which descends from the hill. There are also many ice cream vendors. But most of all, in the area of the church, there are people who sell postcards and other memorabilia of the apparition. At Medjugorje, as at Lourdes, you cannot stop the commerce. It is not the doing of the people who live at Medjugorje, but of people from elsewhere. There are no great runners without sweat.

The important thing is the great current of prayers, confessions, conversions, and actions of grace which extend, with-

The crowd praying in front of the rectory on the fifth anniversary.

out limitation, inspite of the lack of places to eat or to lodge. The people without places to stay spend the night on the floor of the church or in the fields which surround it. In the village guest houses, it is the same overcrowding in the rooms and even in the gardens, when weather permits. There are numerous cars and buses which travel to the hotels in the nearby town (20 or more miles away) or even to the Adriatic coast.

The lack of facilities for the pilgrims has been improved to a certain extent. Eight water taps were installed in 1985, as well as benches and picnic tables in front of the church. A building for toilets, of which the pits were dug out this winter with a bulldozer, are in the process of being completed. One of the two sides was usable even though the workers quit before finishing the second. Vulgar news, but good news. I never understood very well how these thousands of people resolved this inevitable necessity without ruining the environs of the church, which remain irreproachable.

One can partly understand, for, if you stay at the church after the evening service, a team of several sisters along with a number of benevolent people all armed with pails and brooms put everything in order in the church. Others clean the surrounding areas. Heroic times are part of history, but they live in obscure and hidden heroisms.

On the evening of June 24, 1986, I was present during the apparition in the rectory. Certain people had led me to hope that, after the intervention of Rome, which stopped the sword of Damocles which had hung over Medjugorje, the apparitions would be able to be resumed in the sacristy room of the church. Previously, this is where the apparitions took place, which allowed the integration of the apparitions to the daily liturgy. Certain Bishops had suggested that this would be able to be done, but the Bishop of Mostar maintained his restrictive orders in all their rigidity.

The apparition of June 24, 1986 (the anniversary of the first day of the apparitions when the seers only saw, from a distance from the bottom of the path, the silhouette of the Virgin on the hill), was not marked by any particular message or event. It is this evolution of the visions which bothers historians of the apparitions. On June 24, 1981, the seers were surprised, astonished, and did not dare to believe their eyes. Today, (five years later) they have learned to let themselves be absorbed by the one who appears to them. The rest of the world disappears to their eyes, without altering the suppleness of their kneeling position nor the tranquility of their faces. The ecstasy does not disfigure them, it transfigures them.

That same evening, June 24, 1986, the prayer group which formed around Ivan and Maria, and often gathers together on Mt. Krizevac, let it be known that all of the pilgrims were invited to join them at 11:30 that night on the hill. The news ran fast and thousands of people assembled there. Everybody knew that this evening would end with a second apparition, but for Maria only, because Ivan is now in the Army at Ljubljana, and Vicka, convalescing, was no longer able to climb the hill. The thousands of pilgrims plodded up the rocky path full of brambles and rough stones. The best equipped had flashlights with them which outlined, on the hill, the thread of the path and the large size of the crowd. There, uniformly, in total discomfort among the plants and the rocks, the silence and the prayers under this limpid sky were intensified. After the apparition, which closed with a prayer, Maria transmitted this message from the "Gospa", which was quickly translated and circulated in several languages:

> "You are on Tabor. You receive benediction, strength and love. Bring this to your families and to your homes. To each one of you I grant special blessings. Continue in joy, prayer and reconciliation."

The next day, June 25th, was the real anniversary date of the apparitions; the day (in 1981) when the group of six seers was defined and they climbed the hill for the first time to see Our Lady up close. For the 5th anniversary, however, they were disbursed: Maria and Jakov were at the rectory; Vicka was convalescing in her home; Ivanka was at her home for the first of the annual apparitions that has been promised to her; Ivan had simple "locutions" in his barracks; and Mirjana was praying without seeing like the other pilgrims.

The evidence of this anniversary shows a strong continuity of grace, conversion and of prayer, which grows without fever or spiritual greediness. If there are signs, the people take them as they come. What the pilgrims are looking for are the essentials, and that is what had maintained Medjugorje in spite of impossible conditions.

Chapter 2

HOW TO PAINT AN APPARITION

Several days before the 5th anniversary, the Belgium painter Leopold Baijot had come to Medjugorje to present the picture of the apparition that he had painted, after long and tenuous meetings with the seers, and much discerning prayer. It constituted an event because of the special care of this undertaking, which we are now going to talk about. It may be the first time that a renowned international painter had the courage to challenge this seemingly insurmountable problem: How to paint an apparition.

The difficulty of this problem is like trying to make a square out of a circle. Not only does the painter need to paint what he does not see, but what the seers see is revealed from another world, in another state, which transcends painting. History shows how difficult this problem is. For example, the sculptor Fabisch, who the ladies of Delacour had engaged, for a royal contract of 7,000 francs of gold, to make a statue conforming to the apparition at Lourdes, questioned Bernadette conscientiously, but she was disappointed with the result. It was merely impossible. The artist is a creator. He plies, with great difficulty, these intangibles described to him. But most of all, he throws himself at the impossibility of translating the ineffable.

For more than a year, Leopold Baijot consecrated himself entirely to this work. He created a painting, and the picture he made was not to sell but to be given. He knew about the traumas of the things that have gone before.

It was the same with the statue of the "Gospa", placed in the church at St. James, and which the pilgrims venerate. On observing the statue, Vicka oscillated between acceptance and rejection. The Bishop originally had the statue removed from the church; it was one of the methods of his plan, of March 25, 1985, to snuff out the phenomenon of Medjugorje.

The painting by the Italian artist, G. Mainardi (page 9),

very well reproduced on postcards by the thousands, had taken on a semi-official allure because it was promoted through the parish. The painter forced himself to translate what was described to him by the seers: "A crown of stars and a pedestal of clouds, a white veil and a gray robe," they said. He conformed to this redundant description. He knew how to create a speaking ambiance in evoking the fields, the blue hills, the church of Medjugorje, under an immense sky that augmented the apparition. This concrete expression speaks to the pilgrims, but, as before with the sculptor Fabisch, the artist had taken certain liberties. He multiplied the folds in the dress and in the veil, which he had blowing in the wind, and the hands of the Virgin seem to indicate something at the left, but you don't know what. And how many stars?

Sunday, June 8, 1985, Leopold Baijot was at Medjugorje at the same time as Sister Briege MacKenna, an American religious known for her astonishing gifts of healing and prophecy. She had predicted, one assures us, of the coming of Our Lady in this place. In praying for the painter, Sister McKenna said to him:

> "You are not here by chance. It is Jesus who sends
> you to glorify Mary. You will make a painting of
> the apparition."

Leopold Baijot was satisfied with this, but did not rush ahead. He took his mission seriously and in prayer. He made several trips to question and interrogate the seers. They are always embarrassed when someone pursues descriptions on this apparition of another world. He appropriated a white veil and had Mirjana place it on the head of his wife and he photographed the result. For the color, he set out a variation of colors from which they were to choose the ones that fit. He asked the seers to pose in order to show him how the "Gospa" positioned herself: In a praying gesture? A praying gesture which looked like it was inviting prayer? For a long time he had been inhibited by the idea of doing a painting which he knew would not be equal to its object. In knowing the stage fright of painters on the edge of creation, I said to him, "Paint, do not come back until you have begun to paint."

When he at last started, at the beginning of 1986, everything went very quickly.

His project seemed able to go along with his figurative and impressionistic style. He finished the work, the most correct to this day, and he did it without sacrificing his credibility. He added neither decoration, nor dramatization, nor contrasts to give relief to the expression. It is a symphony in blue, delicate and fine. The gestures are represented in the exact manner. And he was able to get the number of stars that he wanted. Vicka was surprised when I asked her about this precision. The patient Maria had studied the painting to verify it. It is really the woman of the Apocalypse 12: "A crown of 12 stars."

As soon as it was finished, Leopold Baijot invited me to Belgium to see the work. We began by praying in front of the painting. And it was in praying that I felt the intuition and the intentions of the prayer which had sustained him, and above all, this "look", which made one think of the Icons because the Icons were not made to be looked at; they look at us. He found the meaning of the look. He never pretended to see the apparition. He gives a sign of it in his own particular style.

Rene Huyghe said to him at Liege in 1981, "You are very happily influenced by the Venetian light. It was what Delacroix was missing, who didn't know Venice...Your light is beautiful. You are on the same track as Turner, a painter that I like most of all. One finds in your work what I would call 'the eye of the center'. Were you aware of that?" Baijot was not yet aware of it.

It is in looking at his own painting that he began to understand this interior process which made him build his painting in the arc of a circle, in reference to one impalpable center point. In the painting of Medjugorje, it is the look of the Virgin which is in the center, in the circle of 12 stars and in the oval of the mantle. Baijot was impressed to find in the clouds at the bottom of the painting (which he had painted

The painting by G. Mainardi, reproduced by the thousands and distributed through the parish, is very popular; but the painter did a liberal interpretation.

from instinct) a certain cloud formation resembling a dove, which he had not really intended to paint. He saw in that the signature of the Holy Spirit, and figured that this was an indication to omit his own signature.

Leopold Baijot had regarded his work as a mission with a desire to be exact, which made him make even more trips for information. He had overcome the disaffection of several of the seers, who did not whole-heartedly believe in his project, or who did not know how to answer his questions. He persevered with the two most cooperative, Ivan and Maria, who resigned themselves to answer him up until the end.

The artist himself, desiring to survive this obstacle course, asked for some signs from heaven. He has the feeling of having obtained them.

Such a thing is very respectable and usual in the Christian tradition. But these little providential signs, which we all find on our way through life, are not necessarily to be communicated, and perhaps should not be the object of demonstrating proofs. "Keep them to yourself," I told him.

In all respect to his freedom to do otherwise, I do not think that he would have served his cause, nor that of Medjugorje, in letting other people know about his personal proofs, especially in having them on television.

In March of 1986, wishing to help him, I asked for comments from several of the seers, who had already seen the first sketches of the painting: "Not so smiling, the hands higher," they said.

June 24-25, 1986, around the 5th anniversary of the apparitions, I delivered a photo of the painting, separately, to each of the five seers who had been present at Medjugorje. As I was waiting, the painter himself was waiting, and, as was the case with Bernadette at Lourdes, their first reaction was to say, "That is not it." "You can't do it like that." After that, one listens to their responses, the details, all their extremely varied comments; and even though they do not converge, they do all agree on one point, "She appeared to us alive, warm, communicating." A static painting cannot translate that.

The painting by Leopold Baijot completed in 1986 from the descriptions of the seers. (Reproduced in color on the cover).

It comes down to the fact that the apparitions are not a contemplation of a certain style, "leche vitrine," but of a state, a communication. For example, a child who knows his mother well perhaps would not be able to recognize a picture that one has painted of her, because it does not give the same sense of contact, this exchange, this love that a mother represents for him.

For the rest of the criticisms, they are on pure details, and are not the same with all the seers. Mirjana agrees on the color stating that it is the same as she herself sees. Vicka says that the robe should be more gray (kind of a shiny gray, maybe the silver gray of money, a little more blue). There are also little criticisms about the gesture of the hands. And several would have her more smiling, but it is a matter of choice, because the Virgin is sad when she speaks of sin and the difficulties hanging over the world. All of the seers attest to that.

The position and the number of the 12 stars and several other details are appreciated very positively by the seers. Maria said to me in conclusion, "It is the best, it is the best of all."

In short, this work may be, not only the best picture and the most conforming to the apparition, but the most convincing to this day. The painter in creating it had made use of all the facilities that were available to him, but the apparition was inexpressible. All works of art, by definition, are limited; others, tentative.

When speaking of an apparition, it is hoped that this painting by Baijot would be put into "gemmail." This new type of art, born from the middle of the 20th century, exploits in all depth, the resources in the art of the stained glass window. It captures the transparency of the light, and it is able to give the paradoxical "gray," that which the seers were describing (silver gray with a touch of blue). Art will never be adequate, but it could be a sign which projects itself towards the ineffable reality. Created in prayer, as were all the true Icons, this work of Leopold Baijot has already tapped a current of spontaneous prayer. It is hoped that it will be favorably located in a place suitable for prayer.

Chapter 3

NEWS OF THE SEERS

This chapter will cover news of the seers. There is a distinction between those who still see and those who no longer see on a regular basis, after having received the 10th secret (Ivanka and Mirjana, who were the first to see, have both received the 10th secret.). For the others, the revelation of the 10th secret has been at a standstill for the last two years, except for Vicka who has received only 8 secrets. I asked Vicka about this information, "Vicka, you are late in receiving the 9th secret." She answered me with humor, "No. It is the Virgin who is late with me."

April 22, 1986, she too received the 9th secret.

What has happened to the Seers in these last months?

THOSE WHO STILL SEE
Jakov

Jakov, 15 years old on June 3, 1986, has finished primary school at Medjugorje. He goes to the middle school at Citluk, the county seat. The day that I was there, he was still in class at the time of the apparition. He saw it at his own home upon returning from school.

In September of 1985, he declared his intention of becoming a priest. He thought of entering right away with the Franciscans. But the school year was already beginning. He was counseled to wait for the next year.

On November 28, his thoughts of a vocation had a setback. On that day, Bishop Zanic called him, along with the other seers and some priests, to the Bishop's House in Mostar, in order to denounce one of the Franciscan priests, of whom Jakov thought very highly. Young Jakov was visibly troubled by the Bishop's words, and cried much over this incident. During the months that followed (December and January), the psychiatrists, who questioned Jakov during their routine investigative examinations, noticed his depression. Not knowing the cause, they wondered if it were some chronic problem. However, if they had known, they would have recognized that it was the normal effect of a trauma.

Today, after having been assured that the accusation against this priest was ill-founded, Jakov is over this most unfortunate ordeal, but his vocation is now very much in question. He seems to be heading toward an apprenticeship as a locksmith. To add to this trauma, this year also marked the loss of his remaining parent with the death of his father.

Jakov had been receiving messages on the coming events of the world. These ceased on March 6, 1986.

Ivan

Ivan, who was 21 years old May 5, 1986, left for the military service June 16, 1986, at Ljubljana. The Virgin let it be known to him that he would not be having apparitions in the barracks (which would have posed more problems than in a small chapel), but that he would receive internal communications (locutions) which are of a more discreet character.

Since then, there are no more than three seers at Medjugorje. Vicka is often absent because of ill health. Jakov makes every effort to be there as often as possible to assure, with Maria, a certain continuity of the daily event. Ivan is with them and the priests through sending postcards and letters, expressing his commitment. He is doing well in the military and reacts with prudence and country patience.

How were the last months with Ivan at Medjugorje (October 85-June 86)?

Several times per week, he went to one of the two hills, Podbrdo or Krizevac, with the prayer group, which formed itself around him and Maria. This large prayer group was organized as a result of the apparitions. With them, Ivan exercised a calm and quiet radiance. He guided the group according to the messages received from on high:

—Remain in life where you are, do not look for guidance from other places.

—The opening prayer should be addressed to the Holy Spirit.

—Pray three times a day and make use of every opportunity to pray.

—Pray especially on days of fasting. Fast from television.

—Cultivate silence, the Rosary, and the Bible.

—Let the Mass be at the center of things.

—Do not enter into vain discussions. See and speak only of positive things.

The group continues, guided now by Maria and Vicka.

Up until his departure for military service, Ivan continued to work on the family farm. During the leisure time of the winter, 1985-1986, he worked at helping set up the facilities for the crowds of pilgrims visiting the area. Organizational arrangements and improvements were not authorized by the government. Only detail work had been possible at that time. Since then, the authorities have been more understanding of the needs and allowed the building of some facilities.

Ivan's shyness originally made him flee from the crowds. He did not like to be so visible. He would walk quietly but rigidly to the place of the apparitions.

Since the spring of 1986, however, he would mingle willingly with the crowds around the church. It was at Mary's request that he made this special effort, this witness. Instead of shrinking from the crowds, he is now being a positive force in allowing himself to be seen and recognized.

Has he held onto his project to become a priest? One wonders because he does not seem to be pursuing any particular studies, and, in fact, he seems to avoid them. When he is asked about this, he says that the Virgin has the solution for him. And he is keeping this to himself.

His calm presence is missed at Medjugorje, and is strongly missed by his family. His mother told me on June 25, 1986, "Since he is no longer here, every day seems like a year."

Vicka

Since early 1983, Our Lady has been giving Vicka the story of her life. Vicka is keeping a diary on this, to be released only on Our Lady's command. I saw Vicka again in December

1985-January 1986, and then at the end of March and the beginning of April. She continues to gather, untiringly, around the pilgrims. This is differnt from the other seers, who manage from time to time to retreat from all of this. She remains perpetually available to them, except for the times when her health obliges her to stay in her room.

She doesn't like to speak about her health. If one insists, she answers with the breakout of a smile, "Everything is fine."

In principle, any suffering she experiences is only of her concern. She practices the Mediterranean way to live, present a good face—all is well. However, the psychiatric doctors do not appreciate this, and instead might see in this a symptom of mythomania.

It is difficult to realize all that this independent girl has to put up with in being a sort of guinea pig. When she is questioned or confronted about these things, she is not afraid and knows how to deal with these daily painful little happenings. She is psychologically strong, and can play the game well. She manages to be very graceful and relates well with those around her. Those who come to question her, to control or judge her, do not know how to appreciate this performance. They feel themselves the victim, more often than not, because they cannot lead her to say the things they want to hear. It was the Yugoslavian doctors of those early days (June 27-29, 1981) who best tolerated her manner of speaking while they freely conducted their many sophisticated tests. "Who is not well, me or you?" She asked them.

She knows her limits. She says to Father Faricy, "I will say very happily and voluntarily several rosaries a day, but I am not at all good at contemplation."

That is without doubt because of her personality trait of being very talkative. In spite of this difficulty, she is profound enough, it seems to me. Her transparencies are not superficial. She gives herself without limit to God and to others. She has unconditionally offered her life, suffering and death included, for the intentions of Our Lady, and for the Bishop.

In talking about certain conversations, her responses are lengthy. She relates this story:

"One of the Franciscans of the parish said to me, 'I am sick.' These responsibilities are very heavy for him and he does not see the possibility of taking any free time, which I recommend that he should do. I visited him during his illness, and he said to me, 'If the Lord does not need me, He can take me, but don't let Him prolong this vain inaction.' I told him not to worry, that we will see; and that it is necessary to say 'whatever happens.' "

This "whatever happens" refers to suffering itself, it reveals something of the secret of Vicka. In November, she may have received the advice from Our Lady to no longer submit to any medical treatments. Accordingly, she cancelled a trip to Zagreb, which had already been arranged for her. She then also cancelled examinations of the doctors of the commission, and of others.

Vicka is not afraid of dying. She hopes to rejoin Our Lady who fills her life. But she does fear the end of the apparitions.

"I would prefer not to think about it," she said to Father Bubalo.

Everything happened as if Our Lady could see ahead to this transition. On Januray 6, 1985, the "Gospa" asked her: "If you agree, I will not appear to you for 50 days, and during this time I ask you to accomplish three things."

Vicka is ready to do anything that the "Gospa" asks her. She agrees without hesitation, and begins to complete the three sacrifices requested of Our Lady, that she has not yet revealed.

During this time her health is better, and her complexion flourishes.

On February 25, she came to the rectory for the apparition. Is she worried? No, not at all, but confident. The video cassette attests to that marvelously. She begins to pray with Ivan and Maria, as usual. The apparition is on time. She kneels. All is happiness. Simple, without excess, a happy transparency. She gives herself completely to this communication. Simple gestures, but very expressive. It lasts about 3 minutes. Then she looks up. "Ode!" (Parting) she says, as usual.

This departure leaves Vicka without any sadness; no longer frustrated, but happy. She bows her head and puts her face in her hands.

On April 22, 1986, she received the ninth secret, which seems to be very serious. She cried over it. And Our Lady proposes to her a new interruption of the apparitions, for 40 days this time.

The lack of communication is more severe this time. Her health fails again. She gets very severe headaches and, added to that, the complications from an operation of December 8th, 1984. (They discovered, during the operation for acute appendicitis, a tumor and some intestinal nodules). It was necessary for her to return to Zagreb to consult with the doctors who had operated on her. It was there that she saw the apparition on the 4th of June, the day when Mirjana had another apparition at Medjugorje.

On June 7, 1986, she again had surgery (due to reinfection from her previous operation). She returned home shortly before the fifth anniversary of the apparitions. But she still suffered from complications of her new operation. She could not laugh, because it made her feel worse. I was able to see her several times. She was very thin, but seemed to be resigned to her situation. She was smiling, but she was a little bit transparent. During my visit with her, she was seated on her bed and the conversation was somewhat energetic and enjoyable. The second time, she had to remain lying down. But it was the same smile and the same openness. Even though she does not like it, she let me question her on her suffering. She answered politely, "When these things attack us, we should not let it take over. With love, one can always keep smiling."

During my trip from August 12 to 15, she was resting. The 24th of August, "The Gospa" asked for another interruption, to last 57 days, until October 20th.

Maria

Maria continues to greet the pilgrims, who are principally Italians. Without a book or a lesson, she progressively learned to speak this language with a somewhat limited vocabulary, but with a lot of finesse and a very nice accent.

On December 20, 1985, I asked her, "During the year since last I saw you, what has been the most important thing?" She reflected a minute, perplexed, with a kind of distant smile. then she said, "We are closer to Him."

Her entire life is a testimony. What she is, speaks more than what she says, although she always speaks correctly. The visitors have a feeling of communicating with her inner self, or of finding God through contact with her. The fruits are surprising.

A priest had brought a bus load of Italian pilgrims to Medjugorje, who had come for the first time. They seemed interested but did not confess. After leaving Maria's house, the confessions began. Even though Maria had not spoken of this to them, these people experienced conversion after talking to Maria.

The National Television of Belgrade interviewed her at length, in a report they were doing on Medjugorje, and which was of remarkably good quality and objectivity. It was shown on October 17th in all of Yugoslavia, except the area of Bosnia-Hercegovina, where Medjugorje is located. The simple maturity of Maria showed well on the screen. The reporter questioned her:

> "You've seen a lot of pilgrims? Young people?" He asked.
>
> "Yes." She answered, a transparent and modest smile lights up her responses.
>
> "At your age, there must be one who is closest to your heart?" he said.
>
> "Yes," answers Maria, "And I am very much in love." Her smile brightens.
>
> "The speaker is interested and encourages her, "And his name?"
>
> "Jesus Christ." she says.

The speaker, good at his job, pokes the microphone at Maria with the air of saying, "Hmmm, you got me." For her, it was the cry of the heart, or perhaps the smile of the heart—because Maria does not cry.

She also seems to be able to hold her own against her adversaries, even the Bishop of Mostar. One day he brought her there to criticize the rules of conduct of the priests who believed in the apparitions. She listened politely, then said simply, "But why are you telling all this to me?" It seemed that he could find no fault with her.

A similar critique came from Dr. Belanger, the Canadian parapsychologist (interviewed by the "Sunday Times" magazine October 6, 1985), who cultivated the hypothesis that there was a geophysical force that caused these luminary phenomenon and that they were hallucinations to which the cultural background of the children gave form (the Virgin) in this Catholic country. In other words, the children gave life to the Virgin. But afterwards, in front of Maria, he stated to the Sunday Times, "This extraordinary girl has reversed the entire hypothesis that I have proposed."

THOSE WHO NO LONGER SEE
Ivanka

On the evening of May 6, 1985, Ivanka was in the rectory with Maria, Ivan and Jakov for the apparition. At the end of two minutes, the apparition terminated for the three others. They got back up. Ivanka still sees the apparition. The others were stupified, for they had never seen another of their group in this kind of ecstasy. For Ivanka the apparition lasted for six minutes after which she explained:

> "The Virgin has ended her messages to me on the coming chastisement of the world. She confided to me the 10th secret. Our Lady said to me, 'The apparitions are finished for you, but I will see you again every year on the aniversary of the first apparition (June 25), starting with next year (1986).' She will come to say her good-byes tomorrow at my house at the same time."

"Can we come?" asks Father Slavko.

"The 'Gospa' asked to see me alone." She answered.

It is then alone, that she sees her. Afterwards, she gives Fr. Slavko a note, which begins in this way:

> *As usual, Our Lady arrived by saying, "Blessed be Jesus." I answered, "May Jesus and Mary be forever blessed." I have never seen her so beautiful. She was clothed in the most beautiful robe that has ever been my luck to see. Her veil and her crown threw out reflections of gold and silver. Two angels accompanied her. They were wearing similar clothes. Oh how beautiful it was! I cannot find words to describe it. Only the experience can describe it. Our Lady asks me, "What would you like?" I answered that I would like to see my mother again.*

Ivanka's mother had died in April 1981, two months before the first apparition, and she saw her with the Virgin during one of the early apparitions. Ivanka continues:

> *Our Lady smiled and gives the sign of yes. And suddenly, my mother appeared. She was smiling. Our Lady told me to get up. I obeyed her. My mother held me and then she disappeared. Our Lady then said to me, "My dear child. Today is our last meeting. Do not be sad because I will come again each year on the anniversary of the apparitions, except for this year." (1985).*

The apparition had already told the seers that the anniversary date is June 25 and not June 24 because that first day was only making contact.

According to Ivanka, Our Lady continued in this manner:

> *"Dear child, do not think that you have done anything wrong or that such a thing is the reason that I will no longer come to see you. No, nothing*

like that. You have accepted with all your heart the plans of my Son, and you have answered Him in everything. Few persons on this earth have known this great grace that you and your brothers and sisters have received. Be happy because I am your Mother who loves you. Ivanka, thank you for your answer to the call of my Son. Thank you for your perseverance. Thank you for having stayed with Him for as long as He asked you to. Dear child, say to all of your friends that my Son and myself, we are always near them when they call us. That which I have revealed to you these last years, do not tell anyone until I permit you to do so.''

I then asked Our Lady if I could embrace her. She nodded, and I kissed her. I asked her to bless me. She blessed me, smiling, and said, ''Go in the peace of God.'' She left, slowly, accompanied by her two angels. Our Lady was very happy, very joyful. She stayed one hour.

I saw Ivanka again at the end of December 1985, at Vicka's house. She was smiling, at ease and peaceful. She held up well under the privation of the apparitions. She has arranged to spend less and less time with the pilgrims. She manages to escape and disappear. She is a very hard worker at her house, which is now under her charge since the death of her mother, and because her grandmother is quite elderly.

In February 1986, she attended some spiritual exercises with the other seers. They were divided into two groups: Ivanka and Maria spent three days at Bijelo-Polsge. Ivan, Jakov, and Vicka, somewhere else.

Someone said that Ivanka had received, as did Mirjana, a piece of paper or something, on which were written the secrets. But that was not correct. She told me that around two years ago, well before the end of her apparitions, she received a little code to note the confidential messages that she had received from the Virgin. And since then, she notes them down in this way to protect all their confidentially.

I was there on June 25, 1986, when Ivanka had the first of her annual apparitions promised by Our Lady. She did not have it with the others at the rectory, but in a private manner in a little part of the living room of her family home at Medjugorje. A simple setting, a carpet, two beds and a piece of furniture, mirrored and filled with knicknacks. Many people were in the courtyard reciting the rosary at about 5:30 p.m. She herself had been praying for a long time. Fr. Tomislav began the rosary, preparatory to each of the apparitions; the Joyful Mysteries and then the Sorrowful Mysteries. Ivanka was there, kneeling, wearing a dress with lilac designs on it, a corsage, and a white belt.

I said to myself, with all the critical assessment I could muster because of my work, "What if she does not see anything?" For, after 415 days without an apparition, what would happen? I imagined several possible scenarios, as I observed her.

She was abandoned in her prayers, and without anxiety. At the second mystery, all of a sudden she left the room. Why? Because she had promised her grandmother and two friends that they could be there. It took a few minutes to find them and to bring them in. She then continued reciting the rosary, her face to the back wall, in front of a picture of the Virgin, and lighted by a window.

Just before the apparition, Ivanka turned toward the right wall where the Icon of Linceul de Turin was. She began as before, the "Our Father," and was hardly finished when she knelt down.

The Virgin is there. The calm face of Ivanka is full of happiness. Smiles flood her face. Her lips move but the sound of her voice had disappeared. She speaks only for Our Lady, and then listens, nods her head with conviction several times.

The apparition began at 6:40 p.m. At 6:43 the voice of Ivanka, which had disappeared, comes back to pray with Our Lady. "Who art in Heaven," Ivanka responds.

It is the Virgin who had intoned for her the "Our Father." After this prayer and the "Glory Be," the voice disappears again. Three minutes later the voice comes back to say a second time the "Our Father" and "Glory Be" with the Virgin at her invitation. (It is the only apparition where I have witnessed the double prayer, in contrast to the apparition on February 25 with Vicka, where no prayer had taken place.) For Ivanka, it all comes back, on this night of faith, accentuating the importance of prayer with Our Lady, which is accessible to us all.

Ivanka's voice disappears again. Her profile is serene, very calm. A strand of her long hair hides her eye for all those who see her from the right profile. Her words are more animated now, and filled with smiles.

At 6:54, her head raises very slowly. "Ode," (gone) she murmurs.

The apparition had lasted 14 minutes, after 14 months of absence. In talking with her, I am surprised to find her immediately natural, immediately at ease. She shakes her finger at me to remind me, in reproach, of having tortured her with such difficult questions the day before, but with a sympathetic smile. She is perfectly agreeable to talk, though she wishes for quiet and peace above all else.

Father Tomislav Vlasic comments afterwards, "The Virgin told her several things that were only for her. She spoke to her of secrets, but not a special message. She asked her only to pray much and have people pray. She blessed all those who were there."

"She will see her again next year," concluded Fr. Tomislav, because the next apparition for Ivanka will be on June 25, 1987, and so on until the year 2000, or beyond.

One more time, I was astonished to see the regularity of the progression of these events, so detailed and programmed in spiritual beliefs. It has made itself felt to the seers as well as to me, and my doubt and concerns in asking, "And if she does not have an apparition today?" become superflous.

Mirjana

Mirjana, who was 21 years old on March 18, 1986, continues her studies at the school of Agronomy, In Sarajevo.

In August of 1984, she again felt in her heart the assurance that Our Lady would appear to her once again. On August 25th, according to the promise that the "Gospa" had made to Mirjana (to appear to her during times of difficulty or special need), she appeared for 10 minutes and told her:

"Wait for me on September 13th. I will speak to you of the future."

Mirjana then came to Medjugorje the night before, on September 12th, to her family home located at Bijakovici, opposite Vicka's house. The apparition came to her on September 13, and gave the details of how the secrets should be revealed. Mirjana then gave this information to Father Slavko, the spiritual director of the parish at that time. The message had a very dramatic tone.

"Are you happy to know the future?" Fr. Slavko asked her.

"One word suffices to make me cry all day long," answers Mirjana. "The Virgin is very sad with all the unfaithful people."

"Which unfaithful people? Those who go to church but do not practice their faith, or those who do not know God?" he asks.

"They are both the same," she says. "Our Lady says, 'All adults have the capacity to know that God exists. The sin of the world consists in the fact that they are not interested in God.'"

She states that the prayers and the fastings have diminished the 7th secret. The 7th and not the 8th, she confirmed to me. Certain people hesitated on this number.

A second apparition came at Christmas in 1984, two years after the last regular apparition. It took place at noon and lasted for half an hour. Mirjana tells the story in this way:

"The moment is approaching. A few days beforehand, I will warn a priest. The Virgin will speak to me again at the end of February, but without making herself seen."

The locution at the end of February 1985, took place as foretold, at 8:00 p.m., lasting 20 minutes. Our Lady confirmed to her that she would have her next apparition on March 18, for her 20th birthday, according to the promise of Christmas of 1982 ("You will see me every year on your birthday.")

The apparition on March 18, 1985, took place at 2:00 p.m. It lasted for 15 minutes. It was at Medjugorje. Several people prayed with her.

"After birthday wishes, the Virgin spoke to me of those who do not believe," reported Mirjana. "She told me, 'They are also my children. I suffer for them because they do not know what is waiting for them if they do not convert. Mirjana, pray for them.' "

Mirjana went on, "The Virgin deplores those who are looking for too much money, not only in the parish, but in the whole world. Unfortunate are those who would rather take everything from those who come (no doubt, the pilgrims), and happy are those from whom they take."

Mirjana had prepared 30 questions that she wanted to ask the Virgin that day. Her studies at college taught her how to be methodical. But the apparition stopped the avalanche of questions and said only, "When you need it, you will have the answer."

"The Virgin took the chaplet from my hands," Mirjana recounts, "and told me, 'The rosary is not an ornament for the house as some people let it be. Tell everyone to pray.' "

The next day, March 19, 1985, on the feast of St. Joseph, Mirjana had another apparition lasting 7 minutes.

"It is about the secrets that the Virgin has given to me, but about which I can say nothing," she declares.

In 1985, Mirjana also had other manifestations in the form of locutions (inner talkings, not visions); but she recognized well the voice of the one who had appeared to her more than

500 times (from June 24, 1981, to December 24, 1982). In all, communications took place a dozen times: The end of February at 8:00 p.m.; on March 18 at 2:00 p.m. for 15 minutes; on March 19 for 7 minutes; then June 1 and 15; July 19 and 27; August 11 and 17; October 25; and December 25, 1985, at Christmas.

It was June 25, 1985, that Mirjana unveiled how the secrets will be revealed. This was in response to questions from some Italian pilgrims.

> "The 'Gospa' (Our Lady) has given me a special sheet on which are written the 10 secrets. It is such a type that one cannot describe it. It seems to be paper, but it is not paper. It seems to be silk, but it is not silk. It is visible, you can touch it, but you cannot see the writing. At the right time, I will give this paper, or this thing, to a priest of my choice. He will receive grace to read only the first secret; later the others. My cousin, who is an engineer in Switzerland, examined it but he was not able to identify the material."

Mirjana makes no secret of having this document. But other than her cousin, the Swiss engineer, only another cousin (a girl) and her mother have seen it. This singular point perplexed me, because such a means of revelation more resembles magic than the habitual manner of God, according to the tradition of the Church. It is necessary to be a little reserved on this point. The seers are not exactly infallible.

Other than the three persons mentioned, Mirjana has shown the paper to no one, not even to the priest of her parish.

In June 1985, she still had not revealed the name of the priest who she had chosen to unveil the secrets. We learned his name at the end of August 1985, from Jakov, upon his return from Sarajevo where he visited his father. Mirjana had chosen the young Father Pero (Petar), Franciscan vicar at Medjugorje.

Father Pero says, "I will read the secret 10 days before its realization. After seven days of prayer and fasting, I will reveal it, three days before its happening."

Father Pero took his mission seriously. He fasted more often. He was present at the apparition on October 25, 1985. At that apparition, Mirjana recounts:

> "The Holy Virgin appeared with the greeting, 'Praise be to Jesus.' It is her usual salutation. Again she spoke about those people who do not believe. She said, 'They, too, are my children. I suffer because of them, and they do not know what is awaiting them.'"

> "She showed a great sadness and began to pray for them. The 'Our Father' and the 'Glory Be.' She said that we must pray for them even more. We prayed with her for the weak, for the unhappy, the abandoned. After that she blessed us and then she showed me, as in a film, the realization of the first secret; the troubled state of the world after this first warning; the overthrow of one region of the world."

> Mirjana had cried. She asked the Virgin, "Why so soon?"

> The answer, "Because, in the world, there is too much sin. What can I do if you do not help me? Remember that I love you."

> Mirjana insists, "But how can God have such a hard heart?"

> "God does not have a hard heart," answers the Apparition. "Look around you and see what mankind is doing, then you will no longer say that God has a hard heart."

Yes, man was created free and it is the poor usage of that freedom which has brought about this unhappiness; the utter destruction of man by the bad usage of his own freedom. It has been that way since the beginning. God's justice is not a repressive operation. His justice is imminent. It is the consequence of error and human fault, in a marvelous world that

God has given to our human liberty (*Sir.* 15, 14). The Creator has taken the risk of the freedom, without which there would no longer be any love possible, only robots.

The Virgin questions Mirjana to help her understand, "How many persons come to church, the house of God, with respect and a firm faith and love of the Father?"

"I do not know," answers Mirjana.

"Very few," states the Apparition. "This is a time of grace and of conversion. It is necessary to use it well."

God has placed the happiness and the misfortune of mankind in the hands of man's own counsel. If Mirjana seems to attribute to God the punishments, (which are the intrinsic effect of sin in a world made so well), this mode of expression just negates and shortcircuits. It is the secondary cause, and wellfounded in the Bible. It is mankind's inability to place blame on sin. The young people of Medjugorje speak in a Biblical language, and that invites haughty theologians to use the same indulgence. Salvation is a return to God, who will restore, among His people, more and more order to the world.

"Let us listen to the pressing invitation of our good Mother, Mary," comments Mirjana:

> "After this time of grace will come the time of purification which will culminate with the third warning (or the third secret...the visible sign for all). After this sign, the world will certainly know that God exists. But it will be too late to convert. The encounter with the Heavenly reality will be sad for those who have not profited by the warnings and have not converted. But there will be a great joy for those who have opened themselves up to God in this time of calm."

During the apparition, the Madonna prays two times (in Latin) over Father Pero.

"I was happy because Our Lady was happy with my choice," continues Mirjana. "The heart of Father Pero is completely opened to the Savior. A reward is waiting for him. We prayed with her (the 'Our Father' and the 'Glory Be') for the success of Father Pero in the task which is confided to him."

Our Lady stayed for eight minutes.

"Pray a lot for Father Pero to whom I have sent a special blessing," She says again. "I am Mother, and it is for that reason that I am coming. You have nothing to fear as long as I am there."

November 30, 1985, Mirjana had another apparition, a little shorter than the one of October 25th. The Italian priest, Father Bonifacio, was present. Again Mirjana saw, as in a film, the unfolding of the first message.

"It will be unhappy; it will be a sorrowful sign," she confirmed. "It will come in a short time."

She prayed for the believers and for Father Pero, so that Father Pero will be able to prepare himself for this task.

After the apparition, Father Bonifacio said to Father Pero, "Certain people say that you will not reveal the contents of the secret."

"If I have the right to reveal it, then 10 days beforehand, I will know it, and three days before, I will say it." he answers.

Mirjana had another apparition at Christmas 1985. I met her eight days afterward, on January 1, 1986, at the rectory. I questioned her on this mysterious paper that seemed to be so objectionable for me. She calmly confirmed its existence.

"I can read it, others cannot," she said.

"You showed it to your cousin? Why not to the priest of the parish?" I asked her. I had no answer to this question, neither from her nor from the priests.

"I know all the dates when the secrets will be accomplished," she told me.

She thinks that Rome will recognize the apparitions because of this sign. Here, I fear that she is a bit optimistic, because the signs of God have never had an infallible effect; they are given in a kind of unclear obscurity, which does not force the free will of mankind—the free will which is complex and not preordained. The enemies of Christ were not converted by his miracles, nor even by His Resurrection.

I have tried for a moment, here, to explain the relative difficulties of this surprising scenario, through the apparent Apocalyptic style of Mirjana, so accentuated in the document of November 30, 1983, which was sent to the Pope (and reproduced in my book, "Is The Virgin Mary Appearing at Medjugorje?", page 159). She is the principal inspirer of this.

"Is this just a personal factor with Mirjana?" I ask myself. She gives a message more drama than the other seers. She cries in thinking about the secrets. The others do not. Isn't she just a little bit dramatic? (I had not known yet that Vicka cried in learning about the 9th secret on April 22, 1986.)

I was looking forward to seeing Mirjana more in 1986. Since my interview with her on March 22, 1984, at Sarajevo, it had been very difficult to see her again because she would come to Medjugorje just like the wind, with the hope of passing unnoticed.

When I first met with her in 1986, I was surprised to find a young woman, calm and self-assured. Her speech was relaxed and simple, like the girls of today, but with assurance, intelligence and authority; speaking in relatively easy Italian. Nothing was dramatic in her manner of being; she displayed peace. She no longer had an air of stiffness about her, that she often had in photographs. She has blond hair, blue eyes, a real sweetness and softness; while at the same time a look of force. Her mode of dress was simple without negligence or pretension: blue jeans, violet sweater. Discreet but in good taste. She did not seem at all dramatic. This meeting hardly confirmed my hypothesis which explained the singularity of the messages of Medjugorje by an apocalyptic propensity.

Father Slavko reacts against the alarmist in this way:

> "The Madonna did not come to announce catastrophes, but more to help us avoid them. We all know that a nuclear war is possible, even without apparitions. If a house burns, it doesn't burn because the mother cries 'fire'. On the contrary, the mother comes to save the house which is burning. In that there is hope."

One of the three psychiatrists, who had examined Mirjana in January 1986, told me, "Mirjana is the most mature, the most normal of the seers. She is almost supernormal."

That is saying a little too much, it seems to me. "Normal" suffices. But she seems to be what they say, and my hypothesis has been modified.

"After the sign will be shown," she confirmed to me, "one will be obliged to believe."

"At least those who have good faith?" I suggested. She seemed to approve. "It is not necessary to be afraid of secrets," she added. That surprised me. "But still you cry. They are sad then?" I asked. "Not all," she answered. "Well, if they are so sad, why do you have such confidence?" I continued.

She answered, "The Savior Lord made me to understand. Mary is with us. If we accept her as our Mother, God as Father, and Jesus Christ as Brother, this family will be there for us."

"It is not a happiness of this world? Joy and peace come then from Christ and from the Virgin?" I asked.

"Yes," she said.

Why have the apparitions lasted such a long time? And why such a long time for the revelation of these secrets that you seem to have been announcing for more than a year? Why are they so long in coming?" I asked her.

"Because so many people are taking so long to convert. There have never been so many unbelievers," she answered.

"Then this prolongation has been a merciful delay?" I asked.

"Yes," she said.

Since then, Mirjana has had other locutions. February 15, 1986, the Virgin told her (if I understood what she was saying) that the presence of Father Pero (who was there) would not be necessary at the apparition March 18, Mirjana's birthday.

March 18, 1986, the Virgin appeared and spoke to her again of the coming revelation of the first secret, but she had not shared anything particular about this subject.

26   May 4, 1986, Mirjana had an apparition that lasted for seven minutes, at Medjugorje, in her family home, with Father Slavko and Father Pero. The Virgin told her only a few precise things about the revelation of the secrets, for

Mirjana.

which we are still waiting.

June 23, 1986, I saw the Franciscan, Father Pero, who is charged with the unveiling of the secrets.

"Petar or Pero?" I asked him, since his name goes under both these forms. "It is the same thing," he said, "as Josep or Jozo, or Ivan and Iko. I prefer Petar." It is less harmonious in my French language, but we shall respect the form that he has chosen.

Born in 1946 at Prisaje, Father Petar became a Franciscan in 1967, ordained a priest in 1972, and he became Vicar at Vitina (1972-78), Tihalijina (1978-82), and Seonica (1982-84). Mirjana had chosen him when he was Vicar at Seonica. He had objected at that time by saying, "But I am so far from Medjugorje." However, a little after that, he was transferred to the parish at Medjugorje.

"What was your first impression after you learned you had been chosen for the revelation of these secrets?" I asked him.

"I thought they were kidding," he answered.

"Does this obligation give you any fear?" I went on.

"No, I pray a lot. I do not know why, but I am not afraid," he said.

"Have you seen this paper that Mirjana has?" I asked.

"No," he answered. "However, when I receive the first secret, I will need to fast for seven days, then I will reveal it three days before it will come to pass. I am a little apprehensive about this fast because I am subject to hypertension, but Mirjana tells me that everything will be all right."

I saw Mirjana again, the day after. I was able to ask her a few questions about the place of the first apparition, which I verified with her. I made the same verification with Ivanka and with Milka, Maria's sister. It is very very clear about the location where the first apparition took place when Ivanka and Mirjana were alone.

It is a little less precise about the spot where they saw again that same day, while gathering a little herd of sheep. It was between the bend in the road (where Mirjana and Ivanka were) and a little lower where Milka was. It is not very important because, as Milka explains, for the period of 10 to 20 minutes of the apparition, they moved around and were talking about what they saw on the hill.

I asked Mirjana, yet again, the question about the gravity of the secrets. "But these secrets are not all sad or serious?"

"No," she answered me, smiling. "But most of them are." She insisted again, "If we love God our Father, and Mary our Mother, it is very clear that nothing really bad is going to happen to us."

Father Tomislav Vlasic, who I also met with on these last two days of my trip, confirmed to me, "It would be a complete error to take these messages in only a dramatic or apocalyptic manner. They are an invitation to all to gather together in love, with humility, joy and hope. Humility is important, but without the joy and the hope, it will be misguided. It is a proof of the love, the faith, which we must have."

HELENA SEES THINGS IN A DIFFERENT WAY
Helena (Jelena)

I thoroughly examined the difference between the charisma of the seers and that of Helena, who receives locutions. The seers were given the "grace" of seeing the vision through no doing of their own; this was freely given to them. They received this grace without any preparation on their part.

Mirjana and Ivanka reluctantly admitted something which they do not like to talk much about. During their walk along the hillside, where they had first seen the apparition, they were on their way to smoke some tobacco (they had been working in the fields all day long). This little escapade is something that most all of the children of the village did. It was at this time that they were startled, without warning or preparation, and without merit, by the appearance of the Virgin. The grace of seeing the Virgin has been freely given to them; and it took some time for this grace to be received by them, to permeate them. It was a gradual and progressive process, and they slowly adapted to this ecstasy which gave a whole new dimension to their being, but not without many tears and joltings, especially during those first days.

On the contrary, for Helena it was a "grace" acquired through her participation. For this communication with God, she sacrificed television and other distractions; and she nourished herself with Scripture and Holy Eucharist, and looked for the best conditions to receive it.

Father Tomislav explains, "It was under these conditions that grace grew in Helena; a grace much more profound than that of the other seers. A grace full of fruit and promises, not only for her, but for the others. It is the new daily bread of Medjugorje."

"This charisma is different from that of the Charismatic Renewal," Father Tomislav confirmed to me. "It is a more interior line of development in love, joy, humility of heart, and of silence."

Celebration of Mass at St. James Parish.

The Cross at Mt. Krizevac

Apparition Room at the Rectory

Chapter 4

A PARISH IN TORMENT

One continues to wonder how the parish of Medjogorje continues to function, under these impossible conditions, despite a few improvements and minor changes.

The Sisters for a long time were confined to a small building built out from the rectory. But because of the conditions that now exist, that space is not available. The transferring of the parish store to a little building nearby, have permitted them to recoup a small amount of space in the rectory.

Beseiged by crowds, the parish maintains good order and a quality prayerlife, with a minimum of means, except for the church which was providentially made too big, but which is now too small.

Surprises and unexpected things are never missing there.

From the viewpoint of the civil authorities and of the police, a "modus vivendi" prevails, thanks to the perfect discipline of the pilgrims. The police have never had to watch over a more disciplined and cooperative crowd. Under these conditions, on June 24, 1986, it was openly disclosed that everyone was invited on the hill for the apparition that Maria would have that evening, in the framework of the prayer group of young people. The prayer group meets there one or two times a week. The police certainly knew about this but did not create a problem. Nevertheless, a police helicopter surveyed the hill during the apparitions. It was a discrete way of signaling: "We are always there. The law exists. We see everything." The police knew very well that if they had prevented access to the hill that evening, the discipline of the crowd would have remained intact.

FROM FR. TOMISLAV TO FR. SLAVKO

Events have been a little bit more difficult with the Chancery. In September 1985, Bishop Zanic had Fr. Tomislav Vlasic transferred from the parish at Medjugorje, and installed Fr.

Slavko Barbaric (who had been assisting there) as spiritual director. He assumed the weighty succession in an exemplary manner: "One does not replace Fr. Tomislav," said Fr. Slavko.

Fr. Slavko replaced him without copying him, putting to use his own skills, which were different. But he listens to the same God and the same people. It was a difficult task in many ways. As spiritual director, one of his functions was to work with the cosmopolitan crowds of people from all over the world, speaking many different languages. This task had already absorbed a great amount of his time prior to the departure of Fr. Tomislav. However, Fr. Slavko's presence at Medjugorje was soon threatened for he, too, supported the movement of prayer which the Bishop had decided was over zealous (through a letter of March 25, 1985, addressed to the parish). So, the Bishop had already been making plans for Fr. Slavko's transfer from Medjugorje. But the Franciscan Provincial of Mostar, having difficulty finding a capable replacement (one who could speak several languages) dragged out the execution of this order for nearly nine months.

"I have my bags packed." said Fr. Slavko. "I am ready to leave when the order arrives."

While he was waiting, he assumed, without material means nor additional personnel, other than that of the parish, a task which was comparable to that of being at Lourdes, where more than 100 permanent employees and volunteers assure the numbers necessary to maintain the services provided for the many pilgrims. Fr. Slavko surmounted this mountain of difficulties in the only way possible—prayer and fasting, very strict and often times prolonged. His faith showed through. Often, after being kept up late in the evening by visitors and parish problems, he would get up at 6:00 in the morning to pray in the church during the only tranquil time of the day.

AND TO FR. IVAN DUGANDZIC

On the advice of the Franciscan Provincial, Bishop Zanic named as successor, Father Ivan Dugandzic. It was a good choice. This Franciscan had been on good terms with Bishop Zanic. The Bishop had appointed him a member of the primary, and then the second Commission of Inquiry. He was one of the most esteemed theologians. His judicial influence helped greatly with the work of the original commission, helping to keep their progress on the correct path; i.e., recognizing the fruits of the apparitions. Fr. Ivan Dugandzic was one of the rare members of the Commission favorable to the apparitions (4 out of 13).

He was also spiritual. He was, up until that point, responsible for the formation of the young Franciscans. Intelligent, cultivated, modest; he was endowed with good sense, seriousness and with courage, both spiritually and pastorally. He was neither a leader, nor an orator. Those with these talents, it seems, were transferred, notably Fr. Tomislav Vlasic and Fr. Jozo Zovko, the previous pastor of Medjugorje. (Fr. Zovko was imprisoned by the government for a period of time because of the apparitions.) Bishop Zanic requested these two priests not to preach in this parish, but to restrict their activity to the parishes where they were now stationed.

Fr. Ivan Dugandzic, who hardly spoke any foreign languages, (a little German and Italian, which he perfected from day to day), asked Fr. Slavko, now in a parish some 12 miles away, to come help him communicate with these many and varied pilgrims, which he gladly did. A lay-visitor however, had evidently objected to seeing Fr. Slavko there, and soon after that, the Bishop gave an order to Fr. Slavko to no longer celebrate mass nor preach in Medjugorje.

AN ACCUSATION

On November 28, 1985, the three priests of the parish (Ivan Dugandzic, Tomislav Pervan and Pero) were called to a meeting at the Bishop's house in Mostar, along with the three seers, Maria, Ivan, and young Jakov (who was then 14 years old), as well as Sister Janja, responsible for the community of sisters at Medjugorje, (today transferred as vice-provincial). The Bishop announced an accusation of misconduct against one of the Franciscan priests, formerly attached to the parish. The astonished guests asked, "What has this to do with us?" since the accusation referred to a period many years prior. This suspicion declared against an unsuspecting and presumably innocent man, could not have surprised them more.

The next day, the Bishop of Mostar presented the same report to the Commission. They also were very astonished and asked, "Why are you bringing this up in conjunction with these apparitions?" In the days before and after, the Bishop mentioned the same accusation to several of his visitors. Some were made to feel this constituted a decisive argument against the apparitions.

This apparently ill-founded accusation seemed to bring about a new level of discord between the Franciscans and the Bishop. This latent hostility developed years ago regarding the right of authority for certain parishes and areas of the country, and which had culminated with the suspension of two Franciscans, by the Bishop, a few years ago.

THE PREMATURE DISSOLUTION OF THE COMMISSION

Less than six months later, the investigating Commission, begun by the Bishop in March of 1984, was dissolved without having finished its work. What is the significance of this?

In our "Newsletter" of October 1985, Issue 4, we reported on the fourth and fifth sessions of the Commission and stated that the Commission, investigating the claimed apparitions at Medjugorje, had gained in independence and credibility. Early on, the members had been unfavorable nine to four. The Bishop, had said, "I am sure of a negative judgment since there are nine to four against."

Dr. Mate Zovkic, a theologian from Sarajevo, who the Bishop had chosen to preside in his name at the meetings of the Commission, had been one of the most outspoken adversaries. He held several meetings opposing the apparitions, notably in the diocese of Archbishop Franic, who was favorable to them. At the beginning of one of the meetings, one of the listeners objected, "But our Archbishop is favorable!" Dr. Zovkic answered, "It is because he does not have all the facts to the problem."

The 6th session (September 26 and 27, 1985), finished with

a statement that had appeared in "Glas Koncila" on October 20, 1985. The salient points (with clarifying comments) are as follows:

—One of the members of the Commission had reconstructed the first two months of the apparitions according to the collection of registered written and filmed documents.
—The diaries of Vicka were to be scrutinized. That led to the discussion of the rapport between what the seers had actually experienced and their interpretations of it.
—Reports were given on the fruits of the apparitions since the session of June 24-25, and responding to an inquiry made on the liturgy and the behavior of the pilgrims.
—On September 26, six members of the Commission had gone to Medjugorje to witness the experience of one of the seers, who was alone on that day. On this occasion, two members of the Commission talked with the seer.
—Statements were made that: "The foreign doctors, despite their sophisticated technological methods, disqualified themselves because of not knowing the language of the country."

The 7th session took place on November 29-30, 1985. It opened with the Bishop again bringing up the accusation. The session continued without definitive action, and certain members saw an uneasiness in this session.

The 8th session was scheduled for six months later, in May 1986, and it was at this time that the Bishop announced a negative judgment.

Prior to that (at the end of April), after informing the Congregation of the Faith that a decision had been made, Bishop Zanic went to Rome to present the Commission's findings. On his return by boat, on which some fervent young Italian pilgrims also were traveling, he was questioned by them on the proceedings. He confided that Cardinal Ratzinger did not approve of his methods and he was told not to make a judgment at this time.

The impulsive remarks of the Bishop sometime harden the

content. This could be the case now, to his detriment, because Rome had not said anything against him, and in fact supported him without reserve in his espiscopal duties. After having told him not to precipitate anything, the Congregation of the Faith, in liaison with the Pope (who is following the events at Medjugorje) terminated the Commission which had begun so badly and whose information, without a doubt, is useful but one-sided. The Information will remain secret until the end of the apparition. In case the end should turn out badly, the negative judgment will be able to be pulled out.

May 2, 1986, the Bishop reunited the Commission for the last time at the Bishop's house in Mostar. He received the members at a luncheon in which Fr. Ivan Dugandzic does not participate, so as to remain faithful to the fast requested by the Virgin every Friday. After the lunch, the Bishop requests a secret vote of each one, supported by a written opinion about a page long. Then he declares the Investigating Commission dissolved and the inquiry is then sent back to Rome. It was necessary to send these documents by May 15th, though Cardinal Ratzinger was absent at that time.

What he submitted was evidently a negative judgment. "Eleven were against, two for, and one in doubt." he said to several people who asked, on the following day.

This evaluation is only possible in recognizing that several members who were favorable voted negatively, for the simple fact that they wished to terminate this Commission in order to proceed with future studies of the events.

Other than the success of not permitting a final judgment, the Holy See received valuable information, which included the results of the scientific tests, which shows the seriousness of the events. Where do these scientific works come from? And what significance will they have?

(*Publishers Note:* In January 1987, at the request of the Congregation for the Doctrine of the Faith, a new commission (on a national level) was established to study the events at Medjugorje. This was announced by Cardinal Franjo Kuharic, President of the Yugoslavia Bishop's Conference on January 9, 1987. May Divine Providence guide them.)

Chapter 5

THE SCIENTIFIC WORKS

"As an historian of apparitions, I have studied ecstacies a lot on paper. This was the first time that I saw an ecstacy in reality and, really, this ecstacy stood up to examination very well. There was nothing cataleptic about it, nothing tense or twisted. The visionaries remain quite normal with practically no change in their bodily functions. I was able to have Professor Joyeux, carry out an encephalogram. It is proved that during the ecstacy, the children were not in a dream state. So there is no question of dreams, and still less of epilepsy. This is a very important finding, contradicting many of the explanations advanced in the past.

I could say a lot more about the characteristic of this ecstacy. For example all the young people fall on their knees simultaneously without any signal. At that same moment, their voices become completely inaudible. They have no idea how or why. One just sees their lips moving as they speak to the Virgin, evidently very clearly and distinctly.

When their voices come back suddenly, one hears them reciting, "Who art in Heaven...", and that is strange, the way all start praying the Our Father simultaneously, at this point in the prayer. Now if you ask them why they did not start with the opening words, they answer that the "Gospa" said those words so they all took up the prayer together with the next phrase. At the end of the apparition, one sees how all together, they raise their heads, looking upwards, because the Virgin is disappearing."

(The above is taken from a previous interview with Fr. Laurentin.)

At Medjugorje, for the first time, apparitions have been studied scientifically, by medical technicians with the most advanced medical technology. These works are today published in two independent volumes:

1. Professor Henri Joyeux (with his team) and Rev. Rene Laurentin, "Etudes Medicales et Scientifique sur Medjugorje" (medical and scientific studies about Medjugorje), Paris, O.E.I.L., 1985.
2. L. Frigerio, G. Mattalia and L. Bianchi, "Dossier Scientifico su Medjugorje. Presentazione di Flaminio Piccoli"—President of the Democratie Chretienne (a scientific dossier on Medjugorje—President of the Democratic Christian), a private edition, from D. L. Bianchi, 22010 Gera Lario, Como, Italy, 192 pages, O.E.I.L.

THE LATEST FRENCH AND ITALIAN TESTS

The French studies have been extended, in addition to the book, by a study from a psychological and psychiatric viewpoint, conducted by Professor Cadilhac, along with Professor Joyeux. These tests showed the seers to be of mid-range "normal."

On the other hand, a study on the synchronisms of the apparitions had been done by Madame Henri Joyeux, according to video cassettes of 50 apparitions, resembling my collection. I was looking forward to the study of these synchronisms (to move or occur at the same time; simultaneous) because they are one indication of objectivity. Six synchronisms were observed:

1. The kneeling of the seers at the beginning of the apparition.
2. The disappearance of the voice at the beginning of the apparition.
3. The reappearance of the voice in order to continue the Our Father, begun by the Virgin. (The seers respond in unison: ". . .Who Art in Heaven. . .")
4. Again, the disappearance of the voice at the end of this prayer.
5. The raising of the eyes and the head when the Virgin arises and disappears.
6. "Ode" ("Gone"), the vocalized word signifying her disappearance.

To the above listed synchronisms, two others, which were not observed, can be added and were measured by electro-oculogrammes. At the beginning of the apparition, the ocular globes (eye/pupil) of the seers (which no longer observe the exterior world) do not move; they regain their mobility at the end of the apparition, in about one quarter of a second.

The synchronisms vary, the most often from 1/10th to 4/10ths of a second, according to the variable reaction time of the different seers; Ivanka was the fastest.

There are cases of simultaneous reaction, also, for their reaction to the "Our Father." This is particularly remarkable, since the seers repeat the ". . .Who Art in Heaven" after the "Our Father" is pronounced by the apparition, which cannot be heard by anyone else.

Professor Cadilhac attaches much importance to the study of the "Ode," the word by which one or several of the seers signal the end of the apparitions. "If this "Ode" preceeds the raising of the eyes, you would be able to say it constitutes a signal, which triggers the raising of the eyes and the heads of all the seers," he noted judiciously. Well, this is not the case. The elevation of the eyes and the heads preceeds the "Ode," that one or several of the seers pronounces at the end of this movement. In addition, the "Ode" is pronounced rather irregularly by the seers, either one or another. Of the 50 apparitions studied, 14 times Jakov was the seer to say "Ode" first; Vicka 8 times, Maria 4 times; Ivanka only 3 times, despite her faster reactions with the initial sign of the cross or kneeling at the beginning of the apparition.

Other tests are in process.

The Italian doctors of the ARPA (Association Regina Pacis, presided over by Doctor Farina) have finished an important series of tests which confirm those which we have been able to make.

INSENSITIVITY TO PAIN

The lack of reaction to pain has been studied on people, while experiencing apparitions, since the Middle Ages. The same empirical tests have always been used; i.e., to prick, to pinch, to burn. The Italian doctors were the first to make a scientific study of this. Professor Santini, who has begun specialized research on pain, in the United States, has measured the sensitivity of the seers with an algometer, an electronic instrument which measures the reaction of subjects to a warm stimulus, to something that would be extremely hot. The algometer is a piece of metal that can have the temperature raised to 122 degrees Fahrenheit. The test results showed:

—Without the apparition, Maria and two other seers registered at 3/10th or 4/10th of a second reaction time to stimuli: A normal reaction.

—During the apparition, they no longer registered. Sensitivity to pain had disappeared. The test was limited to 7 seconds; a longer duration could have lead to a severe burn.

Another series of experiments were made on the cornea of the eyes (the ocular globe). The eye reacts to the least amount of pressure; it blinks, it tears. During the apparition, Dr. Santini touched the cornea with a thin piece of nylon, with an adjustable length which permits you to check for accuracy the intensity of the stimulus. This apparatus is called an estesiometer. During the apparition, the seers register no cornea reflex. Cornea sensitivity is therefore completely absent. Blinking the eye (which would be the normal defense reflex) was not produced. It did not happen. Nothing happened.

Tests were also conducted on the seers' eyes regarding reaction to light. This last test, along with others, verified the previous ones conducted by the French team; i.e., during the apparition, there is no reaction of defense against light. A 100 watt bulb had not produced any ocular reaction. These results also confirmed the testings of the Italian doctors.

It is the first time that this insensitivity to pain had been scientifically measured.

ALLUSIONS TO POTENTIAL STUDIES

During the apparition, the ocular nerve and the auditory

nerve are free. The stimulus are normal, but the seers do not react to them.

Dr. Paolo Maerstri, assisted by the engineer Savario Brighenti, studied this progress of the nervous influx, provoked by an ampliphone: Mach 10. They were able to follow the path of the nervous influx, visual and auditory, from the eye or ear up into the edge of the scull (or brain), where the cerebral center decodes and interprets these signs. The ampliphone only follows this nervous influx up to the cortex. To go farther would require heavier equipment. This heavy equipment is not transportable so further studies were unable to be done.

Professor Margnelli explains the test through a simple comparison, "If you dial a number on your telephone, through the number that you call, you create a stimulus similar to that done by Doctor Maestri, projecting a light in the eye or a sound in the ear. The other end of the circuit, the telephone that you have called, corresponds to the cerebral cortex (the gray matter in your brain) made up of nerve cells on which you can put these electrodes to register the effect produced when the stimulus is provided (the ringing of the telephone). A telephone call by itself may not produce that. The telephone rings, but there is no answer (perhaps due to a mechanical disfunction on the line or because no one is there). This is what happens to the seers at Medjugorje. Their consciousness is somewhere else and does not respond."

In short, the seers do not see or hear what is going on around them during the apparition. In addition to that, the nervous influx, visual and auditory, travels in a normal manner to their brain. The rupture, which stops the listening or the vision of the exterior world, is located then somewhere in the area of the cortex, in a point of the brain which cannot be precisely specified. It would require equipment too large to transport to study this effect further.

These numerous tests let us know something about the seers but not about the apparition (the receiver but not the sender). They limit their mode of perception. The hypotheses already developed in "Medical Studies" are confirmed and made more precise in the following points:

1. The perception of the seers shows many signs of objectivity. They see the Virgin not with their hearts, as Helena, but as a living person, in three dimensions; they are able to touch her. Their looks all converge; their conversations with the apparition are coherent for each one, and sometimes for the group when they receive the same message. In short, they have with this heavenly visitor the same type of exchange that takes place in the same way as our reactions and our conversations takes place with a person from this world.

2. However, this perception is not made in the normal manner. If that were the case, all those who are in the room with the seers would be able to see the apparition. A screen was placed between the seers and where they supposed the vision to be, but it did not interrupt the vision.

   The tests confirm, more precisely: They are stimulated by the exterior world, but these stimuli are not perceived by the seers. They are in a state, as an example, of a person absorbed by television who does not even hear the meow of a cat.

   The first series of observations speak of objectivity; the second is inclined toward subjectivity.

3. These two series, apparently opposed, support and agree in the following ways:

   —The perception is not made in the ordinary manner, but in a more immediate manner; the one who appears meets the seers objectively at a more intimate closer level, and normally takes shape in the centers of visual or auditory perception. It is there that these relations of exchange and of conversation takes place.
   —All of these phenomena have a function. The disconnection of the seers with the exterior world conditions this immediate and intimate perception of the person of the other world who appears. The disappearance of the voices (you have talking without sound) protects the intimacy

of the exchanges.

—The convergence of the eyes of the seers places the apparition at about 2 feet above the horizon. All the seers raise their eyes higher as the Virgin disappears in rising.

The seers do not see the apparition as they would see a space vessel coming down from another planet. The distance is not on the order of mileage or light years. It is much more radical than that. It is the distance between our earthly time and a simultaneous time of God. This participation of the seers in another time zone, which comes together all at once, seems to explain some of the peculiarities. The rapture seems to unfold in a very fast manner in comparison with the clocks of our time (especially with Vicka). If the seers speak in a normal pace, it seems that they receive the messages at a much more rapid cadence. The duration of the apparition, which they do not measure, seems indifferent to them. Whether it lasts for 40 seconds or an hour, it seems the same to them.

There is an intersection between our world and the other world (the world of God to which the apparition belongs). And this intersection with the point of our space in time, where the apparition is made manifest, is a required mystery. According to our hypotheses, the disconnection with the world, here, is a condition for the vision of Our Lady, made manifest to the seers. (Who would be able to say that this is not so?) In this hypothesis, all is perfectly coherent. In other hypotheses, you throw yourself on multiple differences. Our explanation is beyond the scientific results of each test.

A RAPTURE SUBMITTED TO A LIE DETECTOR TEST

Professor Margnelli, a neuro-surgeon of the CNR ("Centro Nazionale Ricerche), who specializes in the study of ecstacies and mysterious phenomenon, tested the seers with a multi-lined polygraph, American made (The Diplomat One 1010). This updated lie detector apparently shows secret reactions of the one who speaks in disguising his thoughts.

Professor Margnelli knew, by his former studies, that the rapture takes place with a very strong nerve-vegetated activity.

He therefore tried to explore the functional state of the nervous and vegetative system with this machine. He registered several psychological parameters: cardiac frequency, blood pressure, electric resistance in the skin, the blood flowing in the last flange of the last part of a finger, and respiratory action (in number and frequency).

> "I studied Jakov on September 7-8, 1985, and Ivan on Sept. 9. The most important results concerned the cardiac frequency and the flux of the blood as it goes into the heart. One observes with Jakov a medium frequency of 150 beats per minute, while the blood flow in the 3rd left finger is reduced to a third of that. This reduction of the blood flow provokes acute paleness, dryness, and the lowering of the temperature. It is a question then of a 'hypertonic orthosympathique,' with the closure of the sphincters and the capillaries. The insensitivity of Jakov and of the other young people is therefore complete."

(Sensitivity of the seers is absent during the apparitions.) Professor Margnelli places these raptures of Medjugorje on a path halfway between two extremes:

1. On one part, you have a total cut with the outside world, and
2. The other, the trances where seers remain in contact with the exterior world, and become an intermediary between those who are interrogating and the apparition which responds.

The Professor says, "This was the case of Anna Marie Taigi and also of the seers of Medjugorje during the first apparitions. I noted, formerly (in my report "Medical Studies") that the seers progressively adapted themselves to the rapture. After having taken the part between the apparition and the people who would question them, they gave themselves solely to the perception of the apparition. At the beginning, they responded to the questions of the public and sometimes transmitted the responses of the Virgin. This communication with the exterior world soon ceased as the apparitions continued.

THE RAPTURE ABOVE AND BEYOND
THE PATHOLOGICAL PRESCRIPTIONS

For specialists of trances, such as Prof. Marco Margnelli (author of a book entitled "La Droga Perfetta Meuro Fisiologia Dell'estasi"), Medjugorje has become the source of a renewed scientific inquiry and at the same time a spiritual one.

The study of trances in the past was principally limited to two sources.

1. First, you had the experimental studies made, around the beginning of the century at La Salpetriere, and elsewhere, on the mentally ill. Doctors Pierre Janet (1901) and Charcot defined these trances as a morbid state—hysteria with mystical overtones.
2. Secondly, the literary study of the mystics, made from writings or seen on paintings, but without the possibility of experimental studies. Lacan gives a dissertation on the trance of Therese of Avila in referring to the sculpture that Bernin made of it. Besides these mystic texts, Drs. Henri Delacroix and Henri Bergson had succeeded in recognizing the holiness of the trance, which denotes, among other things, an easy return to reality. The ability to link the reaction to reason was never understood with the mystics.

Medjugorje brings to the doctors, for the first time, some facts that are at the same time accessible to experimentation, and without a pathological character. This last source of information tends to modify the problems and ideas of the rapture that had been previously defined on an insufficient basis. Professor Margnelli has noted the importance of this renewed involvement.

CONCLUSIONS

These medical works constitute a new scientific step: The first medical tests had been realized with some very clarifying consequences:

1. Thanks to these authentic phenomena, one better perceives the freedom and variety of these ecstacies.

   a) Those of Medjugorje have evolved, we have already noted.

   b) The ecstacies of Kibeho (in Africa) are comparable to those of Medjugorje but with these differences: The voice does not disappear when the seers speak to the Virgin. The raptures are much longer. The do not have, as at Medjugorje, a purely contemplative character, but the seers communicate their message or sometimes the oracles to those who gather around them. The seers of Medjugorje come out of the rapture without a transition, in perfect adaptation to the exterior world; whereas the seers at Kibeho fall (without hurting themselves), and pass out in such a manner at the end of the apparition. It takes them several minutes to regain contact with the exterior world.

2. Those who studied the ecstacies had a tendency to characterize them by the state of the most radical disconnection. The more there was a disconnection, the deeper the rapture (this is according to the etymological definition of the word). But if you define a rapture, not by this break or disconnection of being outside of yourself, but by communication with the invisible world, these characters are secondary.

The spiritual quality of one of the seers (Maria at Medjugorje) allows for exception to this communication with a trance where her symptoms are hardly pronounced. Such a rapture may have astonished the specialists of trances, and make them doubt that it was of an authentic nature. But wouldn't this support the illusion which defines the ecstacy by its pathological characteristics?

Dr. Margnelli had already reacted, in his first book, against the definition of an ecstacy through this pathological means. Medjugorje takes it farther in this direction, which is good, from the Christian experience point of view, well recognized by Doctors Delacroix and Bergson.

In the report of this truth of the ecstacy, you have to come to terms with the fact that Jakov, examined by the Italian doctors, presents a considerably accelerated pulse rate. Among the French tests, Vicka presents a similar acceleration, but Maria and Ivanka present a slowing of cardiac rhythm during the ecstacy ("Etudes Medicales," p. 88). These tests are not contradictory, they show the variety of the states of receptivity. Maria, who did not have any acceleration, presents a particular purity of contemplative communication. As far as these accelerations, they seem tied to the communication of the secrets or the messages in some dramatic manner.

During his trip from September 14-19, 1985, Professor Joyeux had the occasion to film, along with Vicka, the ecstacy of a false seer who was slipped in next to her. I show it in my conferences. The difference is astounding between the false seer's exalted, agitated, little coherent gestures and the equilibrium, the alert communication, the transparent beauty that one can see with Vicka and the other seers.

This test also gives credence to the difference between the supernatural which accomplishes nature, and the pathological which disfigures it; between the spiritual and the programmed which finds pleasure in playing (by miming) the appearance of these spiritual gifts.

In short, without entering any more into these techniques, the works of the Italian doctors have confirmed and given us some precise ideas:

1. The insensitivity to pain.
2. The functional integrity of the sensorial paths during the ecstacy (other than the auditive voices, already explored by a team of Professor Joyeux, they explored visual paths).

    Certain interviews have seen in that a contrast, and an indication of the supernatural character of the ecstacy. But

the contrast is not evident, because the mechanism of pain, and that of perception are of their very nature different, this is what Professor Lhermitte told me.
3. The ecstacy is a coherent state which implies a disconnection that is only partial and variable with the exterior world.

Professor Margnelli concludes:

To these young people, the rapture is invincible and spontaneous. It is truly an ecstacy. Normally, an emotional stimulus provokes in the individual vivid and immediate reactions, even if they are short. But for these young people in an ecstacy, neither the normal painful stimulus nor the piece of nylon in the eye, nor all of the other experiments have produced any reactions. The telephone (metaphorically speaking) had, in all these cases, rung on a spirit that was somewhere else. Is it a question then of an authentic ecstacy, comparable in all the other analogues phenomena taken into consideration by the Catholic Church?

TIME FOR THE PSYCHIATRISTS

If the doctors of diverse nationalities have so easily fallen into accord on Medjugorje, it will not be so easy with the psychiatrists. There is a chronic rupture in these two categories. The psychiatrist has a procedure that does not always coincide with that of a medical doctor. The doctor may feel judged by the psychiatrist. The dialogue is often difficult. And so it will be on the subject of these apparitions.

At the beginning of January 1985, three psychiatrists, of three different nationalities, examined the seers. Their report has not yet been made public. They attest to the perfect normality of the seers with slight reserve. We will discuss two or three or them, with some modification.

Bishop Zanic, quick to promote contrary arguments on Medjugorje, released these reservations, even in qualifying Vicka as hysterical, which was only a figurative word in these reports.

He had prematurely discussed them, though it was considered a confidential report. Here are a few observations on these points:

1. Information that had circulated, beginning with conversations which had been mentioned by Bishop Zanic, should be put back into the context of the reports from where they were extracted.
2. The clinical note of hysteria, as formulated by one of the three psychiatrists, relates to the following traits: A propensity to put yourself in the center of something, to capture the eye and the good will of people, etc. But these traits are often found among those people who are professional and who are in contact with the public (as Vicka is daily); i.e., politicians, orators, professors, and the Pope himself. They are not manifestations of an hysterical pathology, even if their activity calls to mind certain traits from this clinical tableau.
3. On the team, even among the three psychiatrists (who worked in liason with the two psychiatrists of the Episcopal Commission) the interpretation of the case of Vicka was far from being unanimous. The three doctors had been able to observe Vicka when she was in one of these states, that her family calls a coma, and that the psychiatrists call a stupor (which is a momentary loss of consciousness). They proposed a psychological explanation of hysteria. But others tend to explain this as a "cyst" on the brain for which she has submitted herself to numerous exams in Zagreb. As long as the psychiatrists do not have access to the medical records, which could show the physical cause of these headaches, it is very risky to trust a psychological explanation.
4. On the psychological and psychiatric level, the Italian doctors, who also examined Vicka, have given out very positive judgments on this questionable point. Psychological tests of Dr. Gagliardi on Vicka seemed to indicate something diametrically opposed to this sense of hysteria:

"During the interrogation, Vicka looks first at one and then at the other, but rarely at the camera. She does not look intentionally at the camera but she does not try to escape it either. There is nothing in her but the desire to respond adequately. In other words, her responses do not reveal an unreal or imaginary situation, but a very realistic world, positive, lived with simplicity and joy. During all the time that we were at her house, we did not observe any neurological signs. Everything came about with extreme simplicity and coherence."

Those, as myself, who have known Vicka for a long time, can only testify to her remarkable, psychological equilibrium, confirmed despite the conditions which could be psychologically dangerous to her life.

The psychiatrists have noticed these risks. It is true that these seers sustain, without protection, risks of deterioration from which it would be advantageous to protect them. But who does not assume risks in some way? The inquisitions of the doctors, and even more so of the psychiatrists, are more traumatic to the seers than the ordinary visitors. Even more difficult, would be the inquisitors of the Theological Commission. Vicka has particularly noticed these differences. To the first doctor, charged to examine her on June 27, 1981, she began by saying, "What examination would you like to make? When I am in need of medical consultation, I will come of my own willingness."

The heart of the problem to the seers, who have voluntarily submitted to so many tests, is entirely different from that of the psychiatrists, professionally solicitous of protecting them. They are testimonies of the apparitions. No one can testify in their place, and the "Gospa" has given them this mission. They have a clear conscience. They have measured the difficulty and have accepted all the consequences. They seem to receive the special graces to surmount this difficult situation.

Having known Vicka and the other seers for a long time, and attentive to their human and spiritual beliefs, I hold them to be quite normal.

Certainly, even with the majority of "normal" subjects, weaknesses are present. Small pathological inclinations exist, even among psychiatrists. But a normal subject is one who recognizes his weaknesses and knows how to make the best of them, in a stable manner, and with steady progress. And such is the case with the seers. It would be advantageous for the psychiatrists and psychologists to recognize this essential element.

Ivan was very introverted. He, who used to flee from the crowds and sometimes would bite his lip with embarrassment, has overcome these fears and deliberately affronts the pilgrims, according to the invitation of Our Lady (as we have mentioned).

Vicka, whose strong extroversion is a handicap in an inverse sense (because she has a tendency to over-express herself), compensates well for this particular characteristic. She controls gracefully her beautiful resources and outgoing nature (the psychologists say).

It would be important, then, to note that the diagnosis of the psychiatrists should include a study of the entire life of the seers; one that shows, through time, their progression into these conditions which have often been traumatic.

It is also necessary to situate them in their milieu—an agricultural environment, unmechanized, perhaps like something you would have seen in France 30 years ago. They do much work with their hands and not with machines. The women still carry, often on their heads or their backs, loads as heavy as themselves. In this natural environment, more primitive than it is Mediterranean, these seers have given mediocre results on analytical tests, established for people who live in the city, trained in modern techniques since their childhood. On instinct, Ivanka has refused some of these tests as being totally strange to her. But if their analytical capacities are less developed than those of a young Parisian, they have a much better adaptation to the reality of living. They manage themselves very well in human relations, which are very difficult and trying in every sense. They have said of themselves, "We are neither better nor worse than others." May the psychiatrists be psychological enough to measure, in all of these dimensions, the human evolution and the spiritual one. In recognition of this, I would go so far as to consider them superior in these complex ways. I notice that they have gifts in different degrees, and in some cases far superior to me. I do not have less esteem for the peasant style, as of Ivan, than for the style of the city girl, as of Mirjana. The peasants are often the seniors, and I have met many of them at Medjugorje. Ivanka's father, or Helena's, Marinko, or others who have always put me up at their homes without question. In this regard, I have always felt very small spiritually before this total giving; and especially with regard to Vicka and Maria whose health made them the more fragile of the seers.

Medical contributions are not closed. They continue and the seers accept them because, in contrast to somewhat savage tests done by certain outsiders without medical qualifications, the doctors respect the person of the seers. They try not to be aggesssive with them, and will only work with them with their willingness.

ECCLESIASTICAL STATUTE OF THE SCIENTIFIC CONTRIBUTIONS

People ask, "Why are these scientific people getting mixed up in this?" Some feel that they get in the way of the normal work of the Episcopal Commission; that they interfere with the restraint requested by the local Bishop for a yet to be approved apparition.

My answer to that is, "No, to the contrary, the norms established by the Congregation of the Faith, February 24, 1978 (3,3) comment on these competent initiatives:

> *The Apostolic See in Rome is able to intervene at the inquiry whether it be with the local Bishop or requested by a 'qualified group of the faithful,' even directly, by reason of the universal jurisdiction of the Sovereign Pontiff.*

The group of doctors and the theologians, who are working on these multi-disciplinary works on the Medjugorje apparitions, answer exactly to this definition of a "qualified group," which was mentioned by the Holy See. It is one of the modes of expression of the "Sensus Fidelium," so honored in the Church.

It has its place, traditionally, in the recognition of apparitions. These, in effect, are never the object of a dogmatic teaching but of a discernment, and always conjecture. At Lourdes, as at Pontmain or at Fatima, a discernment of the faithful preceded that of the priests or the bishop.

The abstract principle that is often stated in these cases; i.e., to wait for the judgment of the Church before becoming interested in these apparitions or making pilgrimages, is erroneous. If no one went to these places where the Heavenly seems to manifest itself, then the authority of the Church would have no reason to preoccupy itself with it, and especially not to have to put forth a judgment about it. It was necessary to make a judgment on Guadalupe, La Salette and Fatima, Beauraing and Banneux, because of the crowds assembling there and creating a lot of attention. The "sense of the faithful" had recognized an authentic message and had gone there. The authority of the Church had only come to verify this spontaneous discernment, and to extract errors that mankind may have claimed as a gift of God. In Lourdes, more than 50 claimed visionaries had to be dealt with after Bernadette stopped seeing (between April 11th and July 11th). The severe inquiries by Bishop Laurence could not make them deny what they had seen, but it did eliminate them. But, it could not eliminate Bernadette.

The new Roman Standards agree with the situation. They foretell the effect of a judgment in two different stages:

1. When an apparition or a private revelation creates a large crowd, a preliminary inquest should be rapidly conducted to see if the "Sensus Fidelium" is not erring. In this case, the authority would have to intervene rapidly to prevent or condemn doctrinal errors, or the dangers of false mysticism.

Concerning this first step then, if the first examination is favorable, the authority should permit public manifestations of the devotion, at the same time keeping a prudent eye on things. This is equivalent to saying that nothing is objectionable.

Briefly, a Bishop is not there as a deterrent whose authority can condition final conclusions. Such is the situation at Medjugorje where the Bishop has no reason to say anything against this exemplary parish happening. It is open to all, according to Christian freedom, which, thanks be to God, rules in the Church.

2. If the evolution confirms the authenticity, the Bishop has the time to prepare his judgment on the supernatural character of these apparitions. (Preamble, 2).

But it is not vital that there be a judgment of authority for an apparition to be received in the Church. The Miraculous Medal, and many others, had made their paths in this way. And the Popes, without engaging their authority, have lent their favor to the faithful who have seen these things and attest to them.

It is not necessary to exaggerate the importance of official recognition of apparitions. This recognition is not infallible. It is proposed as having good reason to believe in it, but the authority of the Church does not oblige one to believe in it. These gifts, destined to renew or stimulate faith and hope in a certain place or time, show the gratuitous grace of God and Christian freedom. These are not vain words. It is important that laws do not stifle these happenings. Such is the profound intuition which commands the norms of the Church in this matter.

May this line of pastoral wisdom and discernment, judiciously traced by Rome, prevail on the Balkan affronts and interferences, which menace this work of grace.

Chapter 6

THE MESSAGES

The messages of Medjugorje, that Maria records every Thursday evening, according to the apparition, are posted in the church and distributed to the public, and by telephone, to many parts of the world. (See Publisher's footnote #1)

These messages provoke the fervor of some, but also the criticism of others. "They are repetitive and monotonous," some people say. "One does not find anything new in them."

Fortunately, one could say, because these messages are not new revelations, but a recall to the Gospel, so forgotten. The function of these messages from Heaven is not to satisfy our small curiosities, but to make our deaf ears understand the essentials, and for us to internalize these things. To better understand these messages, we need to place them on several different levels.

THE BASE MESSAGE:

1. The fundamental message, that Our Lady of Medjugorje addresses to the world in danger, is:

> *The return to God, by faith, by prayer, by conversion, by fasting, by penance and reconciliation.*

This fundamental message has been given nearly since the beginning of the apparitions; it was not made to be inscribed on the walls, but in dynamic touches in the heart, (according to the words of St. Paul, cited in the Introduction, p. xiii).

THE THURSDAY MESSAGES

2. The messages that Maria receives every Thursday, for the parish, and the public, are on another level. They are teachings; they complement the fundamental message of Medjugorje. They are repetitive counsels that a mother, who

is patiently rearing her children, would give. They keep bringing back to light the essentials that have been forgotten:

Conversion and return to God, prayer, fasting which sustains prayer and vigilance.

The Thursday messages of Maria began on March 1, 1984. It would be useful to recall these first. (Note: "Dear Children" refers to the visionaries, the people of the parish, and the "children of God" in the world.)

The First Message, March 1, 1984:

Dear children! I have chosen this parish in a special way and I wish to lead it. I am guarding it in love and I wish everyone to be mine.

Thank you for your response this evening. It is my wish that you always be here in greater numbers with me and my Son. Every Thursday, I will give a special message to you.

March 8, 1984

Dear children! In this parish, start converting yourselves. In that way all those who come here will be able to convert.

Thank you for your response to my call.

(*Your example will inspire those who come here to convert themselves.*)

March 15, 1985

This evening, dear children, I am grateful in a special way for your being here. Adore continually the Blessed Sacrament. I am always present when the faithful are in adoration. Special graces are then being received.

(*Every Thursday evening the faithful worship the Blessed Sacrament after Mass, but this evening it was noticed that many men remained in the church for adoration, although they had worked hard in the fields.*)

March 22, 1984

Dear children! This evening I am asking you in a special

way during this Lent to honor the wounds of my Son, which he received because of the sins of this parish. Unite yourselves with my prayers for this parish so that his sufferings may become bearable. Make an effort to come in greater numbers. Thank you for your response to my call.

March 29, 1984

Dear children! This evening I am asking in a special way for your perseverance in trials. Ponder how the Almighty is still suffering because of your sins. So when sufferings come, offer them as your sacrifice to God.

Thank you for your response to my call.

We will not give you the complete series of messages:

—First of all, because they are regularly published by the organizations listed at the end of this chapter;
—Secondly, because they were meant to be heard and put into practice every week, rather than said again and again; for it is then that they appear to be repetitive. The accumulation of them diminishes the impact of their message.

Transmitting the Thursday messages is a discreet event. After the apparition on that day, Maria, returns to her normal state, looks for the closest table (usually in the little dining room of the rectory), and writes down the message.

I asked her, "How are you able to remember exactly the text, when it is maybe four or five lines long?"

She answers me, simply, "I can. They remain with me."

She writes them right away with great certainty. They are not at all literary pieces, but the invitation or talking of a mother to her children. With hardly any exception, each message begins by this maternal calling:

> "Dear children" or "Dear sons" (this word in Croatian has both a masculine and feminine meaning).

They all end, invariably, by a delicate thank you of Our Lady:

"Thank you for your response to my call."

Some of the Messages, at Random:

July 12, 1984

Dear children! These days Satan is trying to thwart all my plans. Pray that his plan may not be fulfilled. I will pray to my Son, Jesus, that he give you the grace to experience his victory over Satan's temptations.

Thank you for your response to my call.

January 10, 1985

Dear children! Today I want to thank you for all your sacrifices. I thank especially those who come here gladly and have become dear to my heart. There are many parishioners who are not listening to my messages. It is because of those who are especially close to my heart that I give messages to the parish. And I will continue giving them for I love you and want you to spread them by your love.

Thank you for your response to my call.

March 28, 1985

Dear children! Today, I am asking you to pray, pray, pray. In prayer you will experience great joy and the solution to every helpless situation. Thank you for moving in prayer. Each one of you belongs to my heart. I will be grateful to all who begin praying again in your families.

Thank you for your response to my call.

April 25, 1985

Dear children! Today I want to tell you to begin to work in your hearts as you work in the fields. Work and change your hearts so that the Spirit of God may move into your hearts.

Thank you for your response to my call.

May 9, 1985

Dear children! You do not know how many graces God is bestowing upon you these days when the Holy Spirit is working in a special way. You do not want to advance. Your hearts are turned to earthly things and you are occupied by them.

Turn your hearts to prayer and ask that the Holy Spirit be poured upon you.

Thank you for your response to my call.

September 5, 1985

Dear children! I thank you today for all your prayers. Pray continually and pray more so that Satan will be far from this place. Dear children, the plan of Satan has been destroyed. Pray that every plan of God be realized in this parish. I especially thank young people for the sacrifices they have offered.

Thank you for your response to my call.

November 7, 1985

Dear children! I am calling you to love your neighbors and to love those people from whom evil comes to you, so that in the power of love you will be able to judge the intentions of the heart. Pray and love, dear children. In the power of love you can do even those things that seem impossible to you.

Thank you for your response to my call.

January 2, 1986

Dear children! I invite you to decide completely for God. I beg you to surrender yourselves completely and you will be able to live everything I say to you. It will not be difficult for you to surrender yourselves completely to God.

Thank you for your response to my call.

January 9, 1986

Dear children! I invite you to prayer so that by your prayer you will help Jesus to accomplish all that He has planned for this parish. By offerings and sacrifices to Jesus all that He has planned will be fulfilled. Satan will not be able to do anything.

Thank you for your response to my call.

January 23, 1986

Dear children! Again I invite you to prayer of the heart. If you pray from your heart, dear children, the ice-cold hearts of your brothers will be melted and every barrier will disappear. Conversion will be easily achieved by those who want it. You must intercede for this gift for your neighbors.

Thank you for your response to my call.

February 27, 1986

Dear children! Be humble. Live in humility.
Thank you for your response to my call.

March 27, 1986

Dear children! I wish to thank you for your sacrifices and to invite you to the greatest sacrifice of all, the sacrifice of love. Without love you are not able to accept me nor my Son. Without love you cannot bear witness of your experience to others. That is why I invite you, dear children, to begin to live the love in your hearts.

Thank you for your response to my call.

April 10, 1986

Dear children! I wish to call you to grow in love. A flower cannot grow without water. Neither can you grow without God's blessing. You should pray for His blessing from day to day so that you can grow normally and carry out your activities with God.

Thank you for your response to my call.

April 17, 1986

Dear children! You are now preoccupied with material things and in the material you lose everything that God wants to give you. I invite you, dear children, to pray for the gifts of the Holy Spirit that you need now, in order that you may give witness to my presence here and to everything I am giving you.

Dear children, abandon yourselves to me so that I can lead you totally. Do not be so preoccupied with the material things of this world.

Thank you for your response to my call.

May 29, 1986

Dear children! Today I am calling you to a life of love toward God and toward your neighbor. Without love, dear children, you cannot do anything. Therefore, dear children, I am calling you to live in mutual love. Only in that way can you love me and accept everyone around you who will come to your parish. Everyone will feel my love through you. Therefore, today I beg you to start loving with the burning love with which I love you.

Thank you for your response to my call.

June 19, 1986

Dear children! In these present days Our Lord has permitted me to intercede for extra graces for you. For this reason I again wish to invite you to pray. Pray without ceasing. In this way I can give you the joy that Our Lord gives me. With these graces, dear children, I wish that your suffering may be transformed into joy. I am your mother and I want to help you.

Thank you for your response to my call.

June 26, 1986

Dear children! You must strive to realize, in union with Him, an oasis of peace. I desire that you take care of this oasis so that it remains always pure. There are some who through their thoughtlessness ravage peace and prayer. I call you to testify and to help by your own way of living to see that peace is preserved.

Thank you for your response to my call.

August 28, 1986

Dear children! I want you to be an example to everyone in all that you do, especially in prayer and witnessing. I cannot help the world without you. I want your cooperation with me in everything, even in the smallest things. Therefore, dear children, help me by your prayer from the heart and by surrendering completely to me. In that way I will be able to teach you and lead you along the road upon which I have set you.

Thank you for your response to my call.

October 16, 1986

Dear children! I want to show you how much I love you but I am saddened that I cannot make you understand my love. It is why I invite you to prayer and a total abandonment to God, because Satan wants to hold you into the daily things and to take the first place in your life. Also, dear children, pray without ceasing.

Thank you for your response to my call.

October 23, 1986

Dear children! Pray for peace. Without your prayers dear children, I cannot help you in the realization of the message that the Lord has given me.

Thank you for your response to my call.

November 6, 1986

Dear children! Pray for the souls in purgatory. Each soul needs prayers and grace to get to God, to divine love. For that you need to get more and new people to pray. It will help you to recognize that the world is not important for you, but you have to aspire to Heaven. That is why dear children, pray without ceasing, in order to be able to help yourselves and others to whom our prayers bring much joy.

Thank you for your response to my call.

November 13, 1986

Dear children! Pray with all your heart. Change your life day by day. Begin to live a holy life by your prayers and your sacrifices. You have gone to the fountainhead of grace. May she lead you to paradise with the privileged gift of holiness. That is what I desire for each one of you. So change your life to be more holy. I will always be with you.

Thank you for your response to my call.

SPECIAL NOTE:

A significant change has recently taken place in Medjugorje. On January 8, 1987, Our Lady announced that she will no longer be giving weekly Thursday night messages, but instead, will give a message on the 25th of each month.

The following are the last Thursday night message and the first two monthly messages, given to Maria.

January 8, 1987

Dear children! I want to thank you for your response to my messages, especially dear children, thank you for all the suffering and prayers you have offered me.

Dear children! I want to give you messages from now onwards no longer every Thursday, but on the 25th of each month. The time has come when what My Lord wanted has been fulfilled. From now on I will give you fewer messages, but I will be with you. Therefore, dear children, I beg you to listen to my messages and live them so that I can guide you.

Thank you for your response to my call.

January 25, 1987

Today dear children, again I want to call you to begin to live the new life from today onwards. I want you to comprehend that God has chosen each one of you in order to use you for the great plan of salvation for mankind. You cannot comprehend how great your role is in God's plan.

Therefore dear children, pray that through prayer you may understand God's plan for you. I am with you so that you can realize it completely.

Thank you for responding to my call.

February 25, 1987

Dear Children! Today I want to wrap all of you in my mantel and lead you towards conversion. Dear children, I beg you to surrender all your past life to the Lord and to surrender all the evil that has been deposited in your heart. I want each one of you to be happy, but with sin nobody can be happy.

Pray and in prayer you will comprehend a new way of joy. All the joy in your heart will be displayed and so you will be joyful witnesses of what my Son and I want you to be. I am blessing you.

Thank you for responding to my call.

Fr. Tomilsav Vlasic, commented on the messages in his address to a pilgrimage at Medjugorje on Sept. 13, 1984. In part, he stated:

> "It is useless to come into this church to ask if it is true that Our Lady has appeared. It is of no use to know if she has appeared or not. Perhaps a Committee will discuss this question in ten or twenty years' time; it is of no value to confirm whether Our Lady has appeared or not. The value consists in whether we accept Her messages, if we put them into practice and obtain the gift of the Redemption."

THE OTHER MESSAGES

There are additional messages, other than those of Thursday, but most of them do not lend themselves to publication for several reasons:

—Some are secrets, reserved for later.
—Others are communications on certain occasions, (we have cited some in Chapter 3, regarding the seers).
—For the most part, they are given to the prayer groups which multiply and grow in the parish. These are not intended for large distribution because they concern the life of these groups, citing both their weaknesses and needs, which do not concern anyone other than them.

We will mention, later on, a few messages of Helena.

Publisher's Footnote #1

Some of the organizations which distribute the Thursday messages are:

The Center for Peace
P.O. Box 66
Essex Street Sta.
Boston, MA 02112

Sr. Isabel Bettwy
Franciscan University of Steubenville
Franciscan Way
Steubenville, Ohio 43952

The Medjugorje Centre
153 Elms Crescent,
London, SW4 8QQ England

Fr. Bob Bedard
Catholic Renewal Center
Ottawa, Ontario
Canada, K1Y 3P7

Site of the first Apparitions.

Chapter 7

THE SIGNS

1. The Healings

The Bishop and the Episcopal Commission were not overly diligent in the study of healings (much less in research); and among the hundreds of claimed healings, they sought out those which had not persevered. In his "Positio," the Bishop cites four who died from among those who had come to Medjugorje asking for healing, and who had shown proof of a remission. But all people are mortal, and even among the sixty-four healings recognized at Lourdes for a century, almost all are dead today, even though a remarkable longevity keeps approximately 15 of them alive. (T. Manigiapan: "Lourdes. Miracules et Miracules," Lourdes, 1986).

Although we will always have to face the possibility of illusion and deception in the proclamation of a miracle, it is still most important to identify those who have been healed (and who give thanks to this day). A good example would be those who were blind, where medicine can confirm the astonishing and inexplicable character of their healing.

Where then is the investigation of these healings, which for a long time has been neglected?

In the previous reference book "Medical Studies," the chapter on Healing, we have indicated a most studied case: That of Diana Basile, instantly healed after 12 years of suffering from sclerosis (MS), which had caused total ceasation of the right eye, very profound motor difficulties, and other malfunctions including a skin malady. The file, studied at the Faculty of Medicine in Milan, takes into consideration about 150 pieces of information.

Since then, Doctors Frigerio and Mattalia have opened other dossiers, to which they have made reference in their "Medical Studies," published in 1985 (soon to be edited in France, O.E.I.L.). The Italian doctors studied in detail, the three cases claimed by Dr. Stopar from Yugoslavia. They are as follows:

—Maria Brumec; who had a compressive fracture of the vertebra TH 11, and declared an invalid for life. She was healed on the pilgrimage to Medjugorje, August 8, 1983. ("Dossier Scientifico," 1986, pg. 163.)

—Damir Coric; who had internal hydrocephalus, with hemorrhaging and a very poor prognosis. He was healed following the prayer of Vicka, during the summer of 1981. (ib. pg. 164).

—Iva Tole; who also had multiple sclerosis, and was treated in Belgrade and Zabreb without any improvement in her symptons. She was healed on September 13, 1981, at Medjugorje, after the invitation of the prayer of Jakov. (ib. pg. 164-165).

The Italian doctors followed the examinations of healings of the pilgrims from their country, as well. They designated them only by the initials of the person in order to conform to hoped for discretion, and not to risk any anticipated conclusions. Two example are:

—Madam B. de R., affected with an incurable malady of the lymph glands, since 1978.

—Emmanuela N.G., 35 years old, mother of 2 children; she had a cerebral tumor, and claims she was healed.

During an apparition, Maria received a message for this woman, whom she did not know. She looked for her, found her, and said to her:

> "The Virgin has asked me to invite you to pray not only for others, but also for your own healing. You have two children, two sons. You must live, you must not die. This evening I will pray to our Holy Mother in Heaven, particularly for you and for your health. Pray also for the priests, pray for the Church, pray much. This is the message that I give you."

On her return to Italy, the illness had regressed. Her strength had come back, the pain had disappeared. The illness was in total remission.

In this latest edition of my book, I can add here, that a German woman, 33 years old, totally paralyzed in her legs since she was 10 years old, began to walk upon leaving the place of the apparitions. I met her last December 16th. It was on May 12, 1986 that she had been healed. Fortunately, she was in Citluk, only a short distance from Medjugorje. The dossier of her healing is #278 in the parish archives.

Because of the lack of an established medical bureau, healings, for the most part remain unknown, or known largely by rumor and without much verification. (See Publisher's footnote #1)

2. *Luminary Phenomenon*

The luminary phenomenon continues, unexplicably, at the rate of about one or two times a month. They are principally of two sorts:

1. The Cross of Krizevac disappears sometimes, replaced by a globe of light; or a glow with the silhouette which makes you think of the image of the Miraculous Medal, or the globe of the world.
2. Many also speak of solar phenomenon, similar to those of Fatima and the dancing sun.

We cannot yet make a definite judgment on these complex phenomenon. Some elementary phenomenon, (for example reflections of the sun against light, transformation of the sun as a flat disc surrounded by a shining crown, as some see when the sun is setting), may have natural explanations. But others are totally unexplainable; they call for an examination. We will give, in our next chapter, an inventory of facts which were communicated to us in several different manners: By testimonies, by photos, by video cassettes. But since we have not yet found specialists for sufficient examinations of these phenomenon, it would be best not to make a premature judgment on these.

This then, is a current need:

—To encourage those who perceive or note such phenomenon to continue their communicating them to me.

—To request specialists to form scientific teams that have the credentials to study these events. If a team, offering similar guarantees as those of the medical team (which has done the studies on the rapture under the direction of Professor Joyeux), would present itself, these documents will be at their disposition. This would create a program of studies which will be totally interdisciplinary, because the alleged facts simultaneously include photography, optics, ophthomalogy, and the study of cosmic phenomenon (geo-magnetic, ionic, tectonic, and the like.).

(See Publishers footnote #2)

FOOTNOTE

1. Though detailed and recognized accounts of physical healings have not been released at this time, Fr. Laurentin specifically identifies 25 claimed healings in his previous book, ("Is The Virgin Mary Appearing at Medjugorje?") pages 152 thru 159.

2. Professors Emmanuel More, (nuclear physics) and Paul Ameze, (electrochemist), have testified to the radiations at Medjugorje. The results in the course of these studies show two things:

    First, there is no radioactivity.

    Second, Ionization is five to ten times greater than the norm, (on the order of 1,000 positive ions per cubic centimeter and 700 negative ions at the place of the apparitions without any notable change, before, during, and after the apparition.)

    In addition to that, the number of people there, should have diminished this concentration. The same team performed, in November 1986, a new series of tests to assure a greater number of measurements in different places. It seems to have already excluded the fact that this ionic concentration could be the cause or effect of the apparitions, but nothing should be overlooked in the study of the varying conditions since certain parapsychologists have looked from this point of view for an optimistic hypotheses beforehand, (a priori). Tests in November were performed by a team of Climatologists directed by Father Muri.

St. James Church

The Village

Chapter 8

THE FRUITS

The major accomplishments of Medjugorje are its fruits; the most sure signs, according to the Gospel itself. "One knows the tree by its fruits." (*Mt.* 7:16-20).

They abound, but they remain tentatively discreet.

They developed under difficult conditions. The pilgrimage is very uncomfortable, with few facilities. The parish liturgy, at times, has been inhibited with restrictions (See Bishop Zanic's letter of March 25, 1984, published in my "Newsletter" No. 4, p. 27-28). It is indeed astonishing that everything is progressing in peace so well.

You cannot hide these fruits, even though the press media, at times, has reported false or questionable information. Such is still the case with the "Anzeiger," a great periodical of the German clergy, edited by Herder (December 1985, p. 465-466). Believing in the good faith in this periodical, I wrote and requested a correction. The editor refused, stating that the information came from the Bishop of Mostar, as the authority. To this date, no correction has yet been made. The fight against the apparitions is blind.

It is under these difficult conditions that the fruits of Medjugorje ripen.

These fruits are to be found on several different levels and are propagating in abundance, beginning with the lives of the visionaries. The seers have remained extremely normal under very difficult conditions. They are, I believe, leading lives of profound holiness, very simple, and at the same time very natural. I believe they are, more than they might appear to be, the leaders of a whole spiritual movement and this spiritual movement has produced its fruits in the parish.

For example, there is the reconciliation between the two villages of Bijakovici and Medjugorje; where in the past hostility was such that in the 1930's the conflicts even lead to deaths. Now, they are just brothers.

It is the same in the families. These people pray three hours a day, for the most part. Morning, evening, and the daily Mass. And half of them fast once or twice a week. And the fruits of all of this can be seen far beyond the parish. Monsignor Franic, the Archbishop of Split, told me, "These apparitions have had more influence, and have done more for the Church in Yugoslavia, in three years than all our pastoral work as Bishops in 40 years."

And to this, we must add the pilgrims by the thousands, from all over the world, who have come here and experienced spiritual conversion.

THE SEERS

We have already written of the seers in Chapter Three. They continue to believe strongly in the Lord, and in correcting their weak points. They are deepening their spirituality.

Vicka, who suffers once again rather seriously, since the end of February 1985, keeps her smile. Her temperament which is lively and open would have a million occasions to explode if not graced by a remarkable patience. Very few realize the price she is paying. She can easily dissolve in tears, by a critisicm or a suspicion. A certain psychiatrist suspected her of having transferred her apparitions to her home in order to become the center, according to this propensity she has for theatrics. On the contrary, she directs the pilgrims toward the rectory, and goes there when she can. Her vocation is heavily charged by the Cross of Christ, which she accepts without complaint, reticence or regret. Around my last contact with her, she was recuperating from an operation. Seated or lying down, according to how she felt, under the great summer heat, she was always smiling and in perfect forgetfulness of herself. Her life has really been given up to God.

Maria is growing in simplicity. She lives in a deep humility which radiates hope.

Mirjana is a very remarkable case! She had moved from Medjugorje after the last of the apparitions for her. She had lived for almost two years, far from this area in a place where studies were strongly secular. She was under surveillance and marked by the police who restrained her, notably on March 18, 1983 until after 11:00 p.m. It was on that day that she was waiting for the first apparition of her birthday, promised to her by Our Lady. This apparition could have taken place only a little before midnight. Mirjana experienced in her school and in her family itself certain difficulties in which she had to be personally discreet. For these two years of being gone, some people thought that she was drifting away. But she came frequently to Medjugorje, discreetly, calmly, and with a new maturity. She lives in an atheistic and secularized environment, in a large city, and though she is profoundly aware of the ungodliness of her surroundings, she ignores it. She is at peace.

Ivanka cultivates discretion and deepens her faith with a great openness for living.

Jakov, who has become a vigorous adolescent, has withstood setbacks blow by blow (such as that of November 28, 1985, mentioned before in Chapter 3); then the death of his father in 1986. He had already lost his mother in 1983. However, he is succeeding well.

These last three seers protect their private lives with a certain calm and good humor. It is not always easy to question them and to convince them of the usefulness of their responses.

Ivan, who was very timid and had isolated himself from the pilgrims, lately has been vibrant in meeting with them. The "Gospa" had invited him to take his part in the testimony.

THE CHARISMA OF THE SECOND GROUP, HELENA AND MARIJANA

The apparitions have been prolonged by the awakening of new gifts of a more private nature. Since the end of December, 1982, Jelena Vasilj, and Marijana Vasilj, (both born in 1972), have been receiving locutions (that is, messages without visions). (See footnote #1, #2).

In this intense environment of familiar parish prayer, this other means of communication with Christ and Our Lady has appeared. Marijana, more discreet, and perhaps less capable of expressing herself, is part of this new awakening along with Helena. Both have the same family name, but not the same parents, ("Is the Virgin Mary Appearing in Medjugorje?" by Rene Laurentin, 1984 edition, p. 91-95).

HELENA

Helena was 10 years old when these locutions began. She is now 14. She has gone through a period of classic adolescence, where her maturing absorbs all of her energy. She is no stranger to femininity. She often changes her hair style (more or less happily). This is normal. In 1860, at a time when the indications of the Parisienne styles were far away from the province, Bernadette made similar trials with her grooming when she was around 14, even going so far as to putting a piece of wood under her full skirt to give her the look of having a hoop. ("Bernadette Vous Parle" by Rene Laurentin). Helena, with the happy, carefree ease of a young girl, is now in a new stage of budding maturity.

She has learned Italian, almost by trial and error, because of the questions on the part of the pilgrims, who come daily to interview her. She responds with the words that she knows, and resolves linguistic problems with a smile and an expressive gesture when the right words are lacking to her.

On June 24, 1986, I congratulated her on her progress in Italian. She is learning more every day.

She is neither timid nor loquacious. She responds in a calm, modest, precise manner, with profound and carefully thought out answers.

A woman, anxiously preoccupied with converting her husband, asked Helena what to do. Helena answered, "Pray only. It is God that converts, not you."

Intelligent, sensible, she was always a good student and her psychological tests are more astute than those of the other seers (except for Mirjana). She is well ahead of her age.

"I would have done badly in trying to do a prayer program as she does them," said Msgr. Franic, Archbishop of Split, looking at the format for a novena before Christmas 1984.

Below is how she recently expressed her experience before a group of Italian pilgrims who had come to question her:

"When I heard that some young people of Bijakovici had seen the Virgin on the hill of Podbrdo, I believed right away; and a little afterward, I began to go to church every evening. I was always attracted by prayer. One day I asked with great ardor, 'Lord, how happy I would be if I were able to believe in You alone.' I prayed to the Lord to give me this, and that I would be able to recognize it. . .

"One day at school, I heard a sweet and clear voice inside of me. 'It is 11:00 o'clock.' It really was 11:00 o'clock. I didn't attach much importance to this, not knowing where this voice came from. Then I heard it more often, and from what it said, I felt sure that it was the 'Gospa' (Our Lady), who was speaking to me, and I began to pray. My friends came around me and we all prayed. One day during our recitation of the Rosary, the Virgin said to me, 'This is not the prayer.'

"We were thinking that we had missed a word. But it was not that. What were looking for was not coming. Instinctively, we began to read the Bible, and to meditate and to pray. Then once again the voice made itself heard. And it said to me, 'Like that, that is good.'

"The voice guided me more and more often. It exhorted me to be at peace with all, to liberate myself from bad habits. I became more obedient. I helped more often at home. That was very astonishing because before that I had been considered as kind of lax in that area."

People often ask me, "How do you see the Madonna?"

"I see her with my heart, inside; all clothed in white and I hear her voice very clearly. Sometimes I do not even need to hear her voice because in thought I recognize what she is saying to me. When I ask her something, I don't always have to say the whole sentence. It is not necessary that her response tell me everything either. When she looks at me, I understand interiorly the response. I feel this interior voice only during prayer, and it is in prayer that I have received the response to several of the things that I have asked for."

Helena's family is remarkable: six children, the last born at the beginning of June 1984. Helena is the second child. The grandfather and the grandmother also live at their house, which was built at the foot of the hill of Mount Krizevac. Grgo, her father, and Stefica, her mother, are solid workers, profoundly united and people of faith. They ordinarily go to Mass every day. He has a lot of class, intelligence, finesse, personal contact, the things that are usually associated with an educator. Helena admires her father, and he admires Helena, but without showing it. He maintains a smiling countenance, but is firm, and a little bit reserved in his ways.

"My father is strict, but I accept it." she says.

Grgo, like most of the men of the village, should have left for Germany, to make money for his family. But he knows how difficult and often destructive this is for a marriage. He succeeds in raising his family on his own place with his little garden.

It is not easy because his house is often a center for visitors. The little domestic touches are often disturbed. Those who receive the hospitality do not always think of helping out. This is the case of a French couple who lived there for a whole month and compensated them with these words, "You will not need to work, God will provide for all your needs." They do not hold any belief in this illusionary prophecy.

Grgo has found an area of his farmland which he was able to make into an outdoor shrine, where Helena could pray with the visitors.

Below are a few responses made by Helena in different circumstances. In the prayer group, December 7, 1985, the eve of the Feast of the Immaculate Conception; she transmitted this message:

When I cannot resolve my problems, I go to Jesus. He has helped me so much. You have to give yourself entirely to him. He always helps.

To Father Remo, January 1, 1986 (reproduced in "Eco"):

When you confide your problems to Jesus, everything becomes easy. On this Christmas, I feel so much love. Jesus ought to be born in our hearts, the "Gospa" told me.

The new year that we waited for yesterday, you have to gather it with peace, with love.

Jesus said to me, "At midnight, I am coming and I am giving the world much peace. You don't feel my presence when you come near me? Where are you then, when I come to give you peace?"

This peace, it is not only accomplished in words, that is not a true peace, but it is a peace in our heart.

Question: You prayed last night (December 31) until midnight?
Helena: Our group prayed from 4:00 in the afternoon until 5:30. Then we went to Mass from 6:00 to 7:30. Then, we joined a large prayer group until 10:00 that evening, and then I came home. We waited until midnight and we prayed one hour with our friend.

To Fr. Bianchi, November 11, 1985:

Question: When do you feel the presence of the Madonna?
Helena: Jesus and the Madonna, I feel their presence several

times every day and always around 4:00 P.M. during the prayer meeting of our group. I have also felt their presence this morning during Mass. The Madonna told me yesterday that she and Jesus are particularly happy that one had prayed so much.

Question: What did the Madonna recommend?
Helena: Prayer, Holy Mass, confession, the seven Our Father's, Hail Mary's, Glory Be's and the Creed. Our prayer should be a prayer of love, to gather the infinite love of Jesus for us.

Question: The Madonna, has she told you about the future?
Helena: No, not revelations about the future. She has only told me, "I often give signs."

Question: What prayer does she recommend?
Helena: The Rosary, the Rosary of Jesus (the traditional prayer of the parish, in the honor of the 33 years of His life). But above all, she wants prayer from our heart.

Question: How does your group come together?
Helena: There is a little group and then there is a big group. In the little group there are 14 of us. With me there is Marijana, who is my age. Jesus and Mary also speak to her. There are a man and woman who are adults. But the others are all young, more or less like me. Jesus and Mary have us follow an itinerary of Christian formation. They guide us also by Marijana. She is my friend, and she is less known than the other seers. We gather in the basement of the rectory or on the mountain of Krizevac, or in our houses. Even more than the Rosary, we put forth prayers from our heart.

Question: Do you write what the Madonna tells you?
Helena: Yes, I write everything.

Question: Do you believe that humanity will be able to be saved?
Helena: Certainly, and in spite of everything.

To Fr. Bianchi at the Beginning of 1986:

Question: What connection do you think there is between the message of Fatima and that of Medjugorje?
Helena: Of Fatima, the "Gospa" has not spoken to me. The true Christian should never be afraid.

Question: The Madonna, has she suggested that one make a consecration to her Immaculate Heart?
Helena: She says to make a consecration to the Hearts of Jesus and of Mary. She has given two prayers and invites all to pray them.

Question: What does she say about the state of the Church today?
Helena: I had a vision of the Church today where Satan is looking to cause trouble for God's projects. It is necessary to pray.

Question: Satan is then working harder than ever against the Church?
Helena: Satan is able to, if we let him. But prayers take him farther away and give difficulty to his projects.

Question: What do you say to the priests who do not believe in Satan?
Helena: Satan exists. God would never bring all this evil to His sons. It is Satan who does it.

Question: Why do you think there is this new aggression of Satan today?
Helena: Satan is a tempter. He looks for ways to turn everything into evil.

Question: As a priest, I ask you: What message is the Virgin bringing to families?
Helena: As a family, they should pray in the morning and in the evening, but also during the day so that their work will be good.

Doctor Mattalia (another questioner) asked, "The Madonna, does she encourage us also to do concrete thinks like to write books, to make studies on Medjugorje as we have done?"

Helena: Today there are a lot of books and very few prayers.

Father Bianchi: What is the greatest sin?
Helena: When man feels great by pride, to feel that he no longer needs anyone. Today, all the people of the West, in Europe and America, think that they are able to do everything alone, without the aid of God. The "Gospa" has said this from the very first of the apparitions.

Father Bianchi: Our Lady of Fatima has asked us to pray for the conversion of Russia. Has she made a similar invitation here?
Helena: One would say that the Russians are perhaps better than the Americans, because they live under an atheistic government, and are not able to do anything; but the people of Russia are good. If the Madonna had not appeared to us, who knows, we would have continued without a doubt as before.

Doctor Mattalia: Thank you, you have responded harshly but justly. (He is referring to the words that she has said relative to the books and the studies.)
Helena: It is the inspiration of the "Gospa."

PRAYER GROUPS

The prayer group which has formed around Helena and Marijana, meets every day around 4:00 in the afternoon, during the winter; in the evening, after the daily liturgy service, during the summer. They sing, they receive interior messages from the Virgin or from Christ; from Christ more frequently, since the end of 1985. The messages critique the weak points of the group, invite them to go beyond, and engage in a more profound union. It is a coherent education, in a life in union with God, and with love.

"Christ speaks to us in a strong manner. He invites us to look to Mary as our Mother," Helena said on January 2, 1986.

This group has formed around Helena since August 27, 1984; young girls her own age. Helena thinks that several among them receive the same grace as she and Marijana (locutions and visions through their hearts).

Another group (60 persons of all ages, who go back to the date of May 1983) come together three times a week, in the undercroft (basement) of the rectory, with Father Tomislav Vlasic. The quality of the participants is remarkable.

The third group, begun in June of 1983, gathers around Ivan (and often Maria) to go to pray on the hill, often on Monday and Friday. Ivan and Maria then have a new apparition. This group also gathers sometimes with some of the pilgrims. Ivan receives messages for the group.

There are other groups too. One discerns here a profound spiritual belief. Vocations form slowly, deeply. It is a return to the Church which is being prepared.

THE PARISH

The parish has undergone the proof of the duration: Five years of fervor. It is difficult to sustain, in a parish weighted down with so many responsibilities, so many difficulties, so many things that were forbidden to them; i.e., the seers are no longer able to take part in the liturgical assemblies. The apparitions are away from the church, and the daily liturgy, for which they were a stimulant, is disassociated from them.

Some of the first guidelines of this life of prayer, of exceptional value, have been taken away, one after the other. With it, the daily life has gone down; habit tarnishes the best of things. But faith is stronger than this ambient degradation.

I had the impression that this "crossing of the desert" has shown a diminishing of attendance at the daily liturgy, a less diligent perseverance of prayer and fasting.

However, the priests of the parish pointed out to me otherwise:

"Yes," they have said, "in this 'crossing of the desert,' you can have a certain statistical reduction, but, in January (1986), at the time when there were not many pilgrims, assistance at daily Mass still counted around several hundred persons. The Church was full. The fasting? Many have without any doubt adapted to this fasting. Those who fast on bread and water two times a week are of a very small number. One time a week is more the thing that is done. But many fast in their own way, according to their temperament, their work, their family life. Since Easter of 1986, many have said to me, 'I have not smoked,' 'I have not drunk.' Other accuse themselves and say, 'I have not fasted.' The preoccupation is the same. This movement of daily austerity is difficult."

This parish continues to be a testimony which speaks and converts. The welcoming and family prayer and rosary edify, in different degrees, those who come.

This exceptional fervor is a new thing for Medjugorje. Religion, undermined by time, by mounting technical material, and the dissuasive action of an atheistic regime, had become fairly sociological. Formerly, the religious foundation of the area had been in a form of recession. This renewed interest is strong for those who have come back to where it all started. The fact that the St. James church had been built in the open field, far from every house, is because of the differences between the villages (there had been a lot of in-fighting in the past between the hamlet and the villages). If they had constructed the church at Medjugorje itself, no inhabitant of Bijakovici would have come there, and the other way around. So, it was therefore built on the plain. People have assured me that this quarrel has had some fatalities. But I have never been able to verify it. These doubtful remembrances have been covered over. The people try not to speak of them. The 87 year old father of Marinko has confirmed to me, on June 24, 1986, the following:

> "Yes, there really were three people killed in the rift between the two clans which confronted each other in regard to the realigning of the borders of the cantons (counties), Ljubuski or Mostar. It was after the construction of the cross at Mount Krizevac in 1933, and before the war, on the spot where they have since built the church. The two opposing groups had been armed with guns. Blows took place. . .all of that is well finished today."

He added, "People have stopped blaspheming. Alcoholism

has stopped and even the quarrels between husbands and wives, families, neighbors. All this has disappeared."

It is necessary and hoped that the same reconciliation will be extended to the differences between the Bishop and the Franciscans. May it end with a peaceful solution that is honorable for everyone.

The religious of Split (Yugoslavia) write: "We now have many vocations here; we don't know what to do with them. The same increase has taken place in the seminaries."

This "effect of Medjogorje" is similar to that which has been noted in Portugal after the apparitions of Fatima, and it is that which had lead Pius XI to grant, in 1930, the first official approval to the apparitions at Fatima.

Father Faricy identifies the root of the phenomenon:

"I studied in depth, through many of the interviews, the spiritual life of these young people. They are very young, but they have a very high quality of prayer. Such a quality is only found rarely in contemplative convents, but these young people have been instructed by the Virgin. She has guided them for more than four years, and after this novitiate, she has spiritually formed them in a way that I have never seen in any religious congregation, in any seminary, or in any convent. It is not only a question of prayer. Their prayer life is prevalent throughout all of their activities. They are always conscious of the presence of the Lord and of the Virgin. They see Jesus in others. They are very open to others. They serve the family and the community. They do everything out of love. And yet, they are very much like the other young people, dressed in jeans, very natural and very normal.

THE PILGRIMS FROM THE ENTIRE WORLD

The fruits are wholesome and durable with the pilgrims. In France, there is less acceptance and pilgrimages to Medjugorje are less; but they are more and more numerous from

Italy, Belgium and elsewhere.

A progression of letters continues to attest to how much these apparitions stimulate faith. The following are a few extracts:

TESTIMONIES

"I keep my pilgrimage as an enchanted souvenir, called to the nourishment of meditations, for a long time. I stayed at the house of a peasant for nearly twelve days, and we have lived nearly a peasant life—crude and pious, these cultivators of the vine and of tobacco... We participated with all the people in the liturgical marathon of the parish; three hours of ceremony every evening in the church bounded by a welcoming warmth; and, in addition to that, Mass in the morning or afternoon with the French group, and add to that our personal prayers in front of the Madonna or on the pathways. You have to take seriously the message of Medjugorje. It has made me, like many others, discover fasting. Our Lady is our mother."

(B.R. to B., June 9, 1985).

"The reading of your book made me go to Medjugorje... That which astonished me was the hospitable sense of the people who were there. I ate in the houses of several village peasants. I approved their hospitality by eating the very last piece of bread with them. What dignity and simplicity in this poverty. What serenity at the house of the seers who have been so besieged by people. How can all of this be sustained without supernatural intervention. Helena had served as an interpreter with the peasants that I lived with. I did not recognize her right away. But I did notice the immense serenity that she radiated, which is not timidity. I saw there more people praying than I have ever seen in my life, me who am hardly capable of praying, and I was not even ashamed. In addition, in reading the "Stabat Mater" in front of the cross at Mt. Krizevac, I cried; something that has not happened to me for years."

(I.S. to Treviso, June 21, 1985).

"Your book has cleared things up for me. It has given me new reasons to love Mary our mother. I decided to go to Medjugorje in September.

> *(L.N.F. to B., Portugal, July 6, 1985.*
> *A similar project from L.N.F.*
> *to Sao Paolo, Brasil, July 6, 1985).*

"Here is the journal of the trip of one of my friends who was with me at Medjugorje. He converted there. He hadn't been to confession for 25 years."

> *(H.F. to P., July 25, 1985).*

"Each time that I read your work, I feel confirmed in that the gift of the Holy Spirit has been given to us by the events at Medjugorje."

> *(L.P.F.R. to V. in Italy, July 31, 1985).*

"That which astonished me, are the testimonies of those who come from there, the attitude of the seers, but most of all of the poor people who pray, who fast, who welcome with so much charity the pilgrims who arrive at Medjugorje. What indifference they have for their own comfort! They are not taken up by money. They have practically nothing, and they seem so happy. It is truly extraordinary. It is for that that I believe with all my heart, but I do not speak so aggressively here at home. I content myself in just passing around the literature and articles to my friends and relatives. It is up to them to judge for themselves however they would like."

> *(Sr. A.B. to T., August 4, 1985).*

"Your book has done much good in the area in which I live."

> *(S. to V., Poland, August 7, 1985).*

"I went to Medjugorje, July 15-16, 1985. What I saw there seemed to be very simple: Prayer, penance, joy, a lot of hidden holiness, lived in the sense of poverty and obedience."

> *(D.A. to N., August 9, 1985).*

"I, who only went to Mass on Sunday, found myself there every day with an immense joy, thanking God and imploring Him for peace and humanity."

(S.B. to Verone, August 11, 1985).

"Medjugorje that we have known since May of 1984, thanks to your information, is a major point in the path of our family and in my professional life."

(Dr. P.D. to A, August 12, 1985).

"The enlistment of silence is getting stronger. I follow you united in the proof that I have been able to understand. I continue to pray and to verify the spiritual fruits of these events."

(J.A., Marseille, August 19, 1985).

"I continue to pray for the victory of Mary. She has already conquered my heart. It is the essentials, and it is through reading your first book, that the light has been turned on in me. That could only be the work of God. May this change in my soul, which has not ceased to progress, this hunger for God, this love of Jesus and Mary, continue to grow in my heart and little by little consume my life. It is not, and could not be, the work of the devil. This peace which is in me chases away the agony and the fear of what is to come. Surely, I have no need of going to Medjugorje (even though I have a great desire to go there) for the messages are enough for me. Daily prayer frees me from sadness. The Lord puts a greater force in me every day. He has triumphed over death. He is revived and living. Good is much stronger than evil. In spite of everything that happens in our world, I have confidence in the triumph of the Lord. This confidence grows unceasingly. . ., stronger than all the rest. And I owe it to Mary. She is the best path which leads us to her Son, the Son of the Father. . . May the Spirit of God guide us and enlighten us. The desire to revolt, which had formerly so taken over me, has disappeared."

(A.G. August 20, 1985).

"I had been at Medjugorje after having read, with much interest, all your writings. Right away, I was taken by the extraordinary ambiance that ruled in this place: Great numbers of confessions out in the open air, the Mass of the parish with such a great fervor... Sunday, August 16, since 4:00 P.M., the faithful of all ages have not stopped confessing out in the open air, in many languages, to numerous priests. The parish Mass around 6:00 P.M. was celebrated in astonishing fervor... After that, the Yugoslavians made the way of the cross, barefooted, up the rocky path of Mt. Krizevac. We saw again this climate of the Beatitudes, present on the mountain, which we had noticed so much last year. We are convinced that all of this could not be founded except on real apparitions, but we are waiting, patiently, for the advice of the Church and the Holy Father. This trip was a very strong time for us."

(G.B. to M., August 30, 1985).

This last testimony was sent to me July 1986 from the United States.

"I am Brasilian, 23 years old. Why have I left my continent for Europe? In May 1985, I read an article about Medjugorje. The message convinced me right away to fast on bread and water every Friday. But it was not enough. In March of 1986, a friend invited me to go to Medjugorje. I was there the 3rd. It is impossible to say what I saw, felt, noticed in this natural atmosphere. I met Ivan, and, as always, he was simple and discreet. This moment has remained with me as in an unforgettable photo in my mind. I have spoken with Maria, at her house, for 20 minutes. Before this simple and pure girl, and because of her questions, I felt moved to give myself entirely to God. That which shone upon me was a life consumed in love. Your book made me understand many things and to grow in the love of God with the Madonna. Thank you with all my heart."

(H.D.G.R., Italy, June 20, 1986).

MEDJUGORJE AT THE PARAPSYCHOLOGY FESTIVAL AT DUNKIRK

Marie-Therese de Brosses, Parapsychologists, ('True Festival' in, "You and Your Future," August 1985, pg. 80) does not hide that the summer festival was dreary except for the unexpected: Someone had brought a sequence of a film, of not great quality, on "The Evening Visitor at Medjugorje."

"The ecstatic and radiant smile of one of the seers, Vicka Ivankovic, born July 3, 1964, was illuminated with a joy that is impossible to describe; a smile on which all the paintings of the Madonna of the Resaissance would be diminished."

The conclusion of the article, at Dunkirk, where only recent films, concerning techniques and manipulation, were shown, said, "The smile of Vicka had been a breath of fresh air. We hope to see there a new trend, and additional films, like this one, but of better quality, that can be made available."

FOOTNOTE

1. Locutions (messages) of the heart; visions of Our Lady after December 29, 1982. S. Barbaric, "Phenomenological Comparative Account of the Inner Locutions of Jelena Vasilj and Marijana Vasilj."
2. In pronunciation through English translation, "Jelena" is often read as "Helena" and "Marija" shows as "Maria."

Vicka.

CONCLUSION

Where Are We Going Now?

Where is Medjugorje Going?

The difficulties which seemed to be driving it to extinction have been overcome. The Marxist government has noted the good order and the non-political tone of the pilgrimages. It has noticed also the benefits for the economy of the country. This Mediterranean country, where life tempers ideology, has been able to find a "modus vivendi," or way of operating (which included two objective programs shown on National Yugoslavian television: one in Ljubljana, and another in Belgrade, October 17, 1985, telling of the apparitions at Medjugorje).

The Bishop, invited by Rome to suspend a negative judgment that he had announced, has faithfully obeyed, and resent to Rome the impromptu and secret advice of its 13 theologians. The doctors of this commission have decided not to take a position.

The quality of the fruits confirms a level which seems to be without equal. It is both solid and sure.

What about the exceptional phenomenon? The apparitions? When will they end? Mirjana has given to us, in a short form, the steps and modalites:

- —First, the revelation of the first two secrets, which have some value as a warning.
- —Next, the visible sign, given for the unbelievers, which constitutes the third secret.
- —Then, the remaining seven secrets (after the first three warnings).

It is this announced scenario which is the problem. One tends to object, "Too beautiful to be true, too precise, and too mechanical in appearance for one to recognize the hand of God. There might be, in this almost too fine a scenario, interferences that the unveiling will manifest. Then, the adversaries could find here motives to triumph. It seems possible, and even probable, that the unveiling will prove otherwise this obscure point of the message.

The 10 secrets of which the seers speak, are they exactly the same? Because of some differences among them, this is not evident. But even any disagreement in the realization of these mysterious steps, does not change anything on the bottom line, which is solid:

A message of urgency for the world, which is morally and materially destructing itself, even more than it realizes.

It is an evangelical means of extracting oneself from this situation. These means, so profound with the seers, must be made a part of our daily lives. It extends into the prayer group, into the parish, with the pilgrims, and in addition to that, on an international scale, to the entire world.

The evangelical message of Medjugorje, the calling to prayer and the giving of yourself are unable to be attacked. I fear that such a demanding level of existence, such an excess of good, will not last; that this too vertical a plan will fall as a plane would fall from the sky when its engines failed.

But, after the 5th anniversary, and through so many proofs, I am reassured, just as I had been for the Church of Poland in the admirable essence of the 60's, or for certain charismatic communities of the 70's.

Let us then be serious, modest, and without vain curiosity, in this time of waiting (strangely fascinating for some) for the end of the apparitions, and let us not forget to remain open to listen to the essentials, which cannot be mistaken.

In all of that, one recognizes the visit and the calling of the "Woman clothed in the sun" (*Apocalypse* 12), who looks after the children of the world, just as she was able, on this same earth, to take charge of the birth of a Child, the Son of God.

THE LATEST NEWS
UP UNTIL THE BEGINNING OF 1987

Since the printing of my latest newsletter (#5), at the beginning of August and up to the end of November 1986, I have made two more trips to Medjugorje (August 12-15, the 12th trip; and October 10-15, the 13th trip). The principle object of these trips was to establish a more precise history on Medjugorje, as well as the collaboration of all the latest news, which follows.

REGARDING THE SEERS

Mirjana

Mirjana had come to Bijakovici for a week, for a new apparition on October 3, 1986, which had been announced to her five months previously. It took place in the presence of Father Pero and five witnesses (not all believers). Our Lady prayed for them. The apparition lasted five minutes.

Our Lady said, "For a long time, I have been calling you to conversion. Continue to pray and to fast."

The new apparition did not seem to provide anything new regarding the revelation of the secrets, which had been detailed in the previous apparition of June 4, 1986. Mirjana had confirmed that the revelation of the first secret is soon, but what does this "soon" mean? It is dragging out to what almost seems an eternity. The apparition had taken place in the house of the Uncle and Grandparents of Mirjana. The house is situated right next to Vicka's. (This house had been enlarged this past summer).

Ivanka

Ivanka was married on Sunday December 28, 1986, to a young man 25 years of age. They have known each other for quite some time and had planned on getting married even before the apparitions. They have waited and reflected. The Virgin had told Ivanka that she was free, and the decision was up to her.

They separated for several weeks to discern their decision. Ivanka seems to have exercised great maturity and patience regarding the future of her life, and appears totally content and at ease with her decision. The ceremony was performed by Fr. Pero, and all the seers, including Ivan, were present.

Ivan

Everything is going well for Ivan in the military service at Ljubljana (not Zagreb, as some had reported). During his first weeks, he had participated in a 500 meter course. He came in first, and that won for him an eight day furlough. He telephoned Mirjana to announce this good news to her. He waited for Christmas to take advantage of this freedom, proof that he assumes his new situation without suffering homesickness. He is more happy in the army than he had been during his two different attempts as a student at the seminary.

He has astonished himself by his performance, at his successes at things that he had never before tried. The calm and the strength that he has developed as a young farm worker had given him the dedication for success. How will he handle this secular success? Will people put him on a plateau with the elite? Or will he benefit from the many fruits with the exceptional aid of Our Lady? Ivan says the latter.

A little after his arrival, one of his superiors said to him, "I know that you have a particular calling. If anybody gives you any trouble because of that, come and speak to me about it."

But Ivan, who probably would have never utilized this recourse, even if things had gone badly, had no reason to use it because everything went well.

At first, he had locutions (interior speaking) almost every day, without an apparition. On Saturdays, he would go to the house of a family friend where, discreetly and without testimony, the Virgin appeared to him. Lately, he has been given permission to go off base in the evening, almost every day, and he has an apparition. So now Our Lady appears to him more frequently.

Jakov

Jakov went to the technical school at Mostar, the school for locksmiths. He is no longer the little Jakov who the Italians found so sweet during the apparitions. He now has a robust character. He has developed more in size than in height. But he is only 15 years old, and he has not finished growing.

He has the voice of an adolescent, a clear look, and is open, vigorous and sympathetic. He is a pleasure to see and will become, without any doubt, a handsome man, who just may have to watch his weight.

Maria

Maria is doing well, both physically and spiritually. During the winter (1984-1985), her excess of fasting, her long meditations, and her work had given indication of some depression, and a slight paralysis, which was thought to be a possible start of heart disease. But, in a neurological exam, this was shown not to be the case. It was a matter of profound fatigue.

Father Slavko asked her to reduce her excessive fast schedule (three times a week) and her long vigils. She assumed, with calm and ease, a very heavy schedule during the summer because Vicka, sick or absent, was not able to receive the stream of visitors. So they came to Maria's house. But she knows how to organize, and has the help of her family and friends.

A little area, outside the kitchen of her home, had been set up for her personal dialogues with the pilgrims. Maria receives, in this courtyard, groups who come one after the other, sometimes as many as 60 people per group. She has help in caring for these people. The pilgrims come to talk with her and ask her questions; she tells them to pray and she prays with them. (She speaks directly to the Italians since she has learned their language.) She does this with a lot of finesse and brevity; she gets right to the point.

Her smile, her simplicity, speak almost more than her words. She becomes more and more transparent, but still functions well with people. With a word, she can often touch hearts. Her receptivity, which made her chosen by Dr. Stopar for his hypnosis experiment, makes her particularly supple to the action of Our Lady. Like Bernadette, she provides a very beautiful and convincing image.

Her task, also, is to transmit, every Thursday, the messages of Our Lady; which are written down, transmitted by telephone and distributed throughout the entire world. She is also responsible for the prayer group which formed around Ivan and herself, and which now rests only on her. And as always, she attends the continuing daily apparitions of Our Lady.

"Your responsibilities are heavy with the departure of Ivan and the sickness of Vicka," I said to her in the month of August 1986.

"Heavy and light," she answers me with a smile. (She added in Croation, words that one of the people there translated for me.) "She was citing the Bible," the person said: "My yoke is heavy, but my burden is light."

She remains active in helping with the work around the house. In spite of the perpetual invasion of visitors, she openly invited me to have lunch in October. Everything was simple, harmonious and without excess; the perfect tact which is done so that the visitor feels at home. Mirjana and Milka, who help her now, cooperated in the kitchen which, while simple, is well furnished. But Milka left in order not to bring any attention to herself. She is becoming very good in Italian, and follows in the footsteps of Maria.

A group of pilgrims took Milka to Fatima, for the 13th of May, and then to Rome July 25th, for an audience with the Pope. The remembrance of her solitary apparition is always present with her.

Vicka

Vicka, who I had visited after her operation in June, 1986, was absent during my trip in August. She spent the greater part of this month away from her home. It was wise to preserve her from this flood of pilgrims, because her generosity does not know how to refuse, but she cannot continue always to accommodate them.

She stayed with a family relative at Trogir, on the shores

of the Adriatic, for a week. She lived in a religious house (a convent) with Sister Josipa Kordic. It was there, one afternoon, that the Virgin appeared to her.

"She put one hand on her shoulder and one on my shoulder," Sister Josipa said to me. "On the return from Trogir," · recounts the Sister, "there was a lot of traffic on the road. These are narrow and winding roads which skirt the sea, and we lost a lot of time. We were not able to arrive at Medjugorje for the right time of the apparition, at 7:00 P.M. in the summer, as was pretold. So we stopped at an orange grove, and there Vicka entered into her rapture. It was very beautiful."

On the original trip to Trogir, Sister Josipa took Vicka, by plane, to Ljubljana as a surprise to see Ivan. They were very happy to see each other. It was then that Ivan confided to her the kind reaction of his superior, so careful of protecting him, even though he did not need it.

A little after Vicka's return to her house, on August 24, 1986, she had an apparition at 1:00 P.M. that was unexpected. No one noticed it and she didn't say anything until that evening. In the evening, she explained in the presence of Sister Josipa.

"The Madonna said to me that she wants to ask new sacrifices from me," she said.

"And, what did you answer?"

"I am all ready. Our Lady will tell me about it this evening," Vicka said.

Waiting for the apparition that evening, she was anxious; afraid that this would be the last apparition for her with the revelation of the 10th secret. "Vicka is not well," her mother said.

At 6:45 P.M., she found herself almost alone. The others were at the church. Her sister, Anna, came into the room with her. A couple of Italians were kneeling outside. The Virgin came.

After the apparition, she explained to Sister Josipa, what happened.

"Our Lady asked for a new interruption of the apparitions, starting tomorrow, August 25th until October 20th. She told me that this will be the last interruption—that is to say, that the next interruption will be definitive."

But Vicka remained smiling in spite of all these apprehensions. Sister Josipa, more worried, questioned her, "Then October 20th is she going to give you her last secret? Or is she going to take you with her?

The apparition of August 24th was a relief to Vicka, because during the preceeding apparitions, she did not know exactly what Our Lady wanted. This Sunday night, everything had become clear.

"Tell me if I can help you in anything," Sister Josipa asked again.

"No. That which I have to do, I can do it alone and not with another," Vicka said.

Vicka did not reveal the reason for this new interruption, nor the sacrifice that Our Lady had asked of her. Sister Josipa has the impression that the last of the apparitions is coming for her.

I saw Vicka at a free time during my trip in October. She showed me the path near where the first apparition had taken place, and where she had taken off her sandals. I was able to talk with her, Maria, and Rusika, the older sister of Maria. Rusika remembered very well a few delicate points of the early years.

After having seen Vicka suffering (though still smiling) at the end of June, I was happy to find her in better form this time. Yet, even though everything is going well, she is still struggling.

A group of young people, former drug addicts, who were involved in a treatment program dealing with both physical and spiritual healing, were camped on a family's field a short distance from Vicka's. Vicka often went to visit with them and brought them much joy. Upon their arrival, seeing their many pairs of shoes lined up, somewhat dirty, she washed them all.

The day of my departure, October 14, 1986, she got up at 5:00 A.M. to say the Way of the Cross on her knees, on the rocky path up the hill of Krizevac. In the evening, she was busy cutting the hair of whoever wanted, with her usual humor and dexterity. A French person presented himself. But when Vicka proposed that Jakov should be next, his reply was a pleasant but firm, "No."

On February 10, 1986, the hospital at Zagreb put out the dream and neurological examinations of Vicka, concerning the supposed tumor on her brain. There was some question as to whether she had lost contact with the exterior world since the end of 1982. The hospital admitted the following psychiatric conclusions, which invite you to revise the pathological diagnosis which was given to the public by a religious.

THE PSYCHIATRIC EXAM:

An excellent contact was established with the subject examined. Warm emotion without symptoms of nervous manifestations, nor psychotic.

General Impression:

Not a psychological malady.

Conclusions of the Psychological Tests:

Intellectual development is normal for this age.

Tests Concerning Personality:

The subject examined is a calm person, emotionally stable, but with momentary tendencies to retreat. Subject also showed traits which accentuate altruism, non-aggression, and adaptability on a social level. A personality which is constantly coherent, resolute and assured in personal contacts. A composite of openness, simplicity and emotional warmth.

The subject was at the clinic, more for a need of control, than for any specific problem. The lethargic state seemed a consequence of her headaches and of general exhaustion.

On October 20, 1986, after the 57 day interruption, Vicka had the apparition that was foretold. She had the apparition at her house. Due to her poor health in the following days,

Father Bianchi celebrated Mass in her room on Thursday, October 23rd.

OTHER EVENTS

On July 25, 1986, the Pope gave an audience to a group from Medjugorje—five boys and fifteen girls from a prayer group and 150 others with Father Barnaba Heichich as the tour guide. Their visit was videotaped, which some of you may have seen. The Pope sang with them "The Canticle of the Pilgrimage." Milka, Maria's sister (and one of the seers of the first day) was there. But I do not believe it is true that the Pope received in audience, in 1986, Fathers Tomislav Vlasic and Ivan Dugandzic, as had been reported.

August 5, 1986 was the birthday of Our Lady, according to the communication received in 1984 by Helena. The day was celebrated with discretion and fervor. An exceptionally large crowd of pilgrims was present. There was also a large number of clergy and religious in attendance.

September 14, 1986, the feast of the Holy Cross, Mass is celebrated on the hill at Krizevac. Once again, a new attendance record for the year is claimed; 100,000 people, they say. But, as we all know, these records of crowds are somewhat subject to question.

On September 21, 1986, a group of well-organized Italians, who had been to Medjugorje, had planned a great service of prayer and fasting at the arena of Verona, in Italy. It was expected that 30,000 to 40,000 people would attend. But the Bishops of this area had taken a position against the apparitions, and just 10 days before this event, the Bishop of Verona forbade the priests under his jurisdiction to go. In obedience, two-thirds of the group deferred going—myself included. But it was too late to get the word out, and about 10,000 people were present for the service. It took place modestly, in prayer, in peace, and in good order. But since it was Sunday, it would not have been good to send this crowd away without the Eucharist. So, a priest, after discussions with the local Bishop, received permission to say Mass for those in attendance.

Wednesday, October 22, 1986, Maria confided to Father

Bianchi that the Virgin had granted a rendevous to a prayer group, with Jakov, at 8:30 that evening on the hill at Krizevac. She acknowledged that the pilgrims could attend, and as a result, 8,000 people were on the mountain.

Our Lady's message, "I thank those who are here, for their efforts, for having come so high, and for their prayers. May they be prepared for giving of peace."

Maria said that Our Lady, crying, repeated this message three times, in order to show the very serious threats, actually present, for peace.

THE CHURCH'S POSITION ON MEDJUGORJE

In a public Papal audience in June 1986, the Pope, when asked by twelve Italian Bishops about Medjugorje, had this to say:

> "Let the people go to Medjugorje if they convert, pray, confess, do penance and fast."

A SPECIAL MESSAGE

January 28, 1987

Mirjana received a special apparition lasting about 10 minutes which took place in Sarajevo on January 28, 1987. The Blessed Mother gave the following message to all of us:

> "My dear children, I came to you to lead you to humility of soul and through this to God. How have you accepted me? At the beginning doubtfully, in fear and distrust toward the children I have chosen. Afterwads, the majority accepted me in their hearts and started to carry out my motherly requests, but unfortunately that didn't last long. Whenever I come, my Son comes with me, but Satan comes also. You have allowed him unwittingly to take charge of you and rule over you. Sometimes you understand that

some of your deeds are not allowed by God but you soon supress that. Do not give in, dear children. Wipe away the tears from my face which I pour out as I watch your deeds. Look around you. Take the time to come to God in the church. Come to the house of your Father. Take time for God in your family and pray to God for grace. Remember your deceased; make them happy with Mass. Do not look down at the poor man who is begging for a piece of bread. Do not chase him away from your abundant table. Help him and God will help you through the blessings he gives you. God may answer your prayers. You have forgotten all this, my children.

"Satan has helped you in this. Do not give in! Pray with me! Do not fool yourself into thinking that I am good, but my brother who lives next to me is not good; you will not be correct. I, as your mother, love you and for that reason I warn you. Here are the secrets, my children, this is what people do not know and then when they come to know, it is late. Return to prayer. There is nothing more necessary than that. I wish that our Lord would allow me to explain the secrets to you a little, but already he is giving you too much grace. Consider how much you have offended him. When was the last time you gave up something for the Lord? I will not blame you further, but once again I want to call you to prayer, fasting and penance. If you want to receive the grace through fasting, then let no one know that you are fasting. If you want to receive a grace through giving alms, let no one know but yourself and the Lord. Listen to me, my children, in prayer reflect upon my messages."

WITNESS TO MEDJUGORJE

The following tells of my visit to Medjugorje, Yugoslavia, and the miracle of the sun seen there on Friday, the 4th of July 1986.

Frances (my wife) and I went on the Fatima Travel pilgrimage tour that left the United States June 30, 1986, for Rome, Medjugorje and Fatima. Father Ken Roberts, St. Louis, Mo., was the tour leader and spiritual director. There were 186 people, which included seven priests and six nuns, all traveling on the "Queen of the World" tour plane. Fran and I made this pilgrimage as a form of consecration to the Hearts of Jesus and Mary, and also to become personally aware of Fatima and Medjugorje for our work with the Riehle Foundation. The Riehle Foundation is a non-profit, charitable organization which distributes Catholic books and materials to anyone, anywhere.

After spending two days in Rome, our tour plane arrived in Dubrovnik, Yugoslavia, at noon on Thursday, July 3rd. We traveled by bus to Medjugorje (a three hour ride) arriving in time for the evening apparition and Mass at 6:00 p.m. My first impression was how large St. James Church was for such a small village. The area was clean, rustic, and the people of humble and modest means. Some of us brought necessities with the intention of remaining all night in the village, perhaps even to sleep on the mountain (which some people do). Mt. Krizevac, about 1800 feet high, is directly behind the church, about half a mile away, and on top is a huge thirty foot concrete cross.

It was now close to 6:00 p.m. Confessions were being heard outside along the wall of the church and inside, with a total of maybe ten priests. There must have been about 2,000 people there for the Mass. The church was packed, and speakers have been placed outside the church for the overflow crowd. The rosary being said was beyond description. (The entire St. James parish must have been there. The large number of children and young people was most obvious.) Seven decades were said. Every person there prayed, and loudly. Songs were sung between decades with intense devotion. Meditations, in Croation were given between several decades. Almost all the people were on their knees. The rosary lasted about forty minutes. Fifteen priests concelebrated the Mass as there were pilgrimages from several different countries. The Mass lasted about an hour and fifteen minutes. It was the most moving Mass I have ever attended. Everyone participated in many languages.

From my position in the front of the Church, I could easily see the faces. Deep spirituality was everywhere. The Croation people seemed unbelievably devout. A young Croation woman was next to me, almost always on her knees and in constant prayer. At the sign of peace, I gave her a brown scapular from the bag of religious articles I had brought to be blessed. Her face was ecstatic. We never spoke. After the Mass, the Creed, seven Our Father's, Hail Mary's and Glory Be's were said, followed by a service for the blessing of religious articles. One of Our Lady's messages to the children was that her blessing of articles did not replace the blessing required from a priest. I presented my bag of articles for blessing. Hundreds of people were gathered near the altar. I noticed the same young woman there, kneeling, offering her rosary in one hand, the scapular in the other.

It is hard to describe how spiritually uplifting that Mass and service was. Almost three hours long. The presence of the Holy Spirit was truly felt. The open devotion of the people was overwhelming, especially the young people. There must have been a half dozen different languages being spoken in Mass prayers simultaneously. The Thursday evening message from Our Lady was then read to the crowd. In summary, it was again a call for "prayer."

After Mass that night, I did not return by bus to Dubrovnik, but stayed at the home of one of the villagers, along with a young man from Austria, who could speak Croation. We planned to get up at 5:00 a.m. to climb Mt. Krizevac, and that morning our gracious host was already up at that time to start the day's work, and with a smile and encouragement, she sent us on our way. I brought a bottle of water with me and two pieces of bread, since Friday had become a day of fast there. It was about a mile walk to the foot of the mountain. Along the way, we met and were greeted by many villagers already at work in their small farm plots.

The climb up the mountain is rocky and steep. Stations of the Cross have been placed at points along the way and can be used for rest and prayer. One third of the way up, we came upon a middle aged local lady—she was going up barefooted. Many there do this as added penance. I offered her water. She refused. We reached the top at 6:45 a.m. At the top I found Fanny (a member of our tour group), a very spiritual lady from Pennsylvania; she had spent the night in prayer on the mountain. Also there were four Croation ladies in their seventies, praying the rosary; a group of teenagers from Italy in prayer; and a group of local teenagers singing and praying. You know with certainty that you are in a very holy place. We prayed there for two hours.

After we came down from the mountain, tour groups started arriving from Italy, Germany, Austria and England, as well as our group from the United States. Masses are said all day long in different languages. Fr. Roberts and some of the other priests from our group were scheduled to be in the apparition room that evening, and all our religious articles were being gathered to be placed there for blessing.

In the afternoon, we climbed Mt. Podbrodo, where the first apparition took place. Wooden crosses of all sizes have been placed there, along with banners, scarves, and hankies from different groups, giving it a very spiritual yet eerie appearance. The heat was tremendous that day. But the Lord looked kindly on us and a sudden shower came up while we were on the mountain. With no place to go, everyone just stood there smiling and enjoying the refreshing rain.

By 5:00 p.m., a huge crowd had gathered at the church. Approximately fifteen priests were hearing confessions outside the church, more inside. At 5:30, Father Roberts and others went into the small apparition room where several rosaries were to be prayed. Outside, pilgrims were also saying the rosary, we in English simultaneously with several other languages. I saw Maria and Jakov enter the rectory. At about 6:00 p.m., the rosary service started in the church. Fran and I left the rectory area to go to the church. We walked around the church, toward the rear, facing Mt. Krizevac. Because of the heat, Fran left to go into the church to look for a seat. I was still standing outside at the right rear of the church. I turned to look at the sun as a small thin cloud was passing in front of it. For an instant I could not believe what I was seeing, thinking, Lord, this can't be happening to me. The sun dimmed and it was now silver in color. It was spinning very fast. And then it was pulsating, throbbing, almost looking like a strobe light flashing off and on at great speed. It seemed to be moving forward and back rapidly. I thought, I had to go get Fran, yell to somebody. But I was afraid to take my enes off of it, afraid it would be gone when I got back.

After several minutes, I finally left to go in and get Fran. People were outside everywhere and perhaps some were talking loudly and pointing, I don't know. I couldn't think or focus on any of them. Somehow, I immediately found Fran in the crowded church. We went back to the same spot and I told her to look at the sun. The same thing was happening, except now the thin cloud in front of it was changing color, and sort of reflecting the sun pulsating. Then the cloud became a deep combination of red and violet color. This lasted several minutes. Fran said she saw something happening but wasn't sure what. To her the sun became a silver disk pulsating backward and forward.

Suddenly, the cloud was gone and the sun became so bright you could not begin to look at it at all. We turned to look at the big cross on top of the mountain. It had a huge golden globe around it. Fran said something about it might only be a sunspot from looking at the sun. This seemed to be possible but I had never before experienced such a golden yellow sun spot, and to have it encircle the large cross on the hill was very beautiful. We started to leave to go into the church. I stopped to look at the sun once more. The blinding light was gone. I could stare directly at it. It was pure white and looked like a host. A thin black ring around it seemed to be accenting its shape. It was pulsating. We turned back to look again at the cross on the mountain. The golden globe encircling it was still there. As we got to the front of the church, I noticed a large crowd gathered on the other side of the church, in the shade of the church and where they could not see the sun at all. They were pointing to and looking at the cross on the mountain. I found out later that they too had seen a huge golden globe around the cross.

The Friday evening service was a repeat of Thursday. Eighteen priests participated in the Mass. It lasted until 8:30 p.m. It was a larger crowd than the night before, with as many outside the church as inside.

We returned to Dubrovnik that night, and the next day left for Fatima. Our visit to Fatima too was a wonderful and spiritual experience. On the flight back to the States, a large segment of the time was given to sharing and witnessing by the group over the plane's P.A. system. A great percentage of the people had witnessed the miracle of the sun in one way or another. A number of them testified to a conversion spiritually. Three young men on the tour, all contemplating the priesthood, made such a commitment. Several teenagers on the tour witnessed to a new birth of their spirituality and asked for prayers and help for teenagers who know so little about God. The priests who were present in the apparition room were reluctant to give details about it, only that it was a deeply spiritual experience with a tremendous feeling of peace. Father Ken Roberts then gave his blessing to everyone on the plane.

William Reck
THE RIEHLE FOUNDATION
P.O. Box 7
Milford, Ohio 45150